SELL WHAT'S IN YOUR HEAD

A PROVEN PATH FOR TURNING YOUR KNOWLEDGE OR EXPERTISE INTO A SIX-FIGURE SIDE HUSTLE OR FULL TIME BUSINESS

JACOB SCHMELZER

Copyright © 2020 by Jacob Schmelzer

All rights reserved.

No part of this book may be reproduced in any form or by any electronic or mechanical means, including information storage and retrieval systems, without written permission from the author, except for the use of brief quotations in a book review.

DEDICATION

To my lovely wife, Bethany. You're the love of my life and I realize more every day just how unbelievably lucky I am to have you.

My three little world-changers, Evie, Jack, and Penny.

My siblings Natalie, Geno, and Johnny. Thanks for letting me practice my selling skills on you when we were kids!

And, my wonderful parents, Steve and Kim.

Thanks for putting up with me Mom and Dad…I don't deserve what you gave me but I'll do my best to do something good with it. Love you both!

CONTENTS

Introduction	vii
1. There's A Business In Your Brain	1
2. If I Can Do It So Can You	5
3. The #1 Secret Of Selling What's In Your Head	13
4. The Only Things That Matter	19
5. Market First	23
6. Product Palooza	31
7. The "Hacker" Course Creation Method	37
8. The "Hacker" eBook Creation Method	41
9. Creating A "No-Brainer" Offer	49
10. The "No-Brainer" Offer Toolkit	55
11. The "No-Brainer" Offer Toolkit Continued	65
12. Simple Selling Process Part One	75
13. Simple Selling Process Part Two	83
14. Unsolicited Business Advice From A Grizzled Veteran	91
15. How To Build A List	95
16. Creating A Product Ecosystem	103
17. Dealing With Tech	107
18. Eliminating Limiting Beliefs	113
19. From Hobby Hustler To Business Baron	125
20. Words of Wisdom	133
Appendix 1: The "Sell What's In Your Head" Cheatsheet	137
Appendix 2: How To Do Market Research	141
Appendix 3: "Hacker" Course Selling Method Cheatsheet	147
Appendix 4: Sales Page Crash Course	149
Appendix 5: Selling With Webinars	157
Appendix 6: Why I Chose To Put This Training In A Physical Book	161
Next Steps	163

INTRODUCTION

Ordinary people all over the world are getting paid for what they know. They're gaining freedom, helping others, and building wealth in the process. They're leaving cubicles and dead-end jobs in the dust to chase their dreams and turn their knowledge into best-selling products.

What may seem like an impossible challenge is actually within reach!

And, now it's your turn.

The book you're holding right now will teach you how to become a world-class INFOpreneur if you put it into action.

Here's my promise to you.

If you follow the steps laid out in this book you'll have a viable info product, a proven business model, your first sale, and a *ton of confidence*.

All within the next 30-60 days…

Are you ready?

1

THERE'S A BUSINESS IN YOUR BRAIN

There's a business in your brain. It's true. And LOTS of people want to give you their hard-earned money for what's in your head. You've got a gold mine just waiting to be explored and monetized.

Don't believe me? Just give me a few sentences to prove it.

Did you know your brain burns around 260 calories a day (I'm sure some people's burn less...snarky laugh) and accounts for around 20% of your body's resting metabolic rate consumption?

That's some serious energy output! So what's going on? Well, brain power is REAL power. That bundle of gray matter up there is capable of quite a lot! It's a super-efficient, super-computer.

The whole point of this book is to *get you to use it*.

...to make something beautiful.

...to make something unique.

...to make something that creates value for yourself and others.

...to make something that helps people and makes the world a better place!

What a Rush!

Remember 1849?

Well, yeah, neither do I but...

It was the year of the California Gold Rush. Over three-hundred thousand "49ers" flocked to California because there was, *"Gold in them thar heels!"* A precious resource, just beneath the surface, waiting to be discovered.

In the 21st century, **information** is the hot commodity and the internet is the modern equivalent of the California boom town. Your brain is a gold mine just waiting to be opened up.

But this rush is here to stay.

"According to Stratistics MRC, the Global E-Learning Market **accounted for $165.21 billion in 2015** *and is* **expected to reach $275.10 billion by 2022** *growing at a CAGR of 7.5% during the forecast period. The key factors that are favouring the market growth are flexibility in learning, low cost, easy accessibility, increased effectiveness by animated learning. Moreover, escalation in number of internet users and growing access of broadband pooled with mobile phones with online capabilities are also fueling the market growth."*

E-learning is expected to be a 275 billion dollar industry in 2022. It's simply astounding. But you know what's even more remarkable? In the gold rush, there was actual scarcity. You had to stake a claim. It was about real estate, mineral rights, and finding a vein of ore.

You also had to pack up and physically go to California where danger, deprivation, and ridiculously inflated prices on goods and services awaited you. Today, all you need is a laptop, an internet connection, and a good idea!

In this new rush, the scarcity is only limited by what can be imagined. Your capacity to dream, create, and communicate is your only REAL limitation. Another way to say it is, your only competition is *you*.

You are the product. Your knowledge, experience, perspective, insights, and ideas are a literal gold mine and I'm going to show you how to get that gold out of your head and into the world.

It's hard to believe...but you can literally **sell what's in your head.**

And no I'm not talking about sketchy medical research involving a lobotomy...

I'm talking about selling information!

The world is starving for new ideas. Demand always outpaces supply. You and I are living at the dawn of the single greatest technological and communication revolution in human history. Information can be created, packaged, and distributed with almost zero time lost and minimal expense.

It's a dream scenario! You can extract value from your brain, present it to the world, and get value in return.

Imagine what it would be like to no longer trade time for money working at a job you hate?

Or maybe you're someone with an existing business and you want to grow your profits and impact...

Or maybe you're someone like me who has a job they love but wants to improve their income?

Info products are the perfect mechanism.

How would it feel to go to work (in your pajamas if you want) and love what you do?

What if you could share your passion with others and have them pay (and thank) you for it?

Too good to be true?

I thought so!

But I'm living proof that you can **sell what's in your head.**

And I'm going to show you how…

But first, let's get clear on something.

The WHAT of "selling what's in your head" is incredibly simple.

1. Create an info product like an ebook or course.
2. Put it online.
3. Sell it.

That's it.

But that's not what you really need to know. What you really need to know is HOW.

And that's what this book is about.

But to benefit you'll need to read *and* apply the information being taught.

This book contains a treasure map but to get the treasure you have to follow the steps and be willing to DIG!

If you do that you'll gain an incredibly valuable skillset that will allow you to create wealth by selling what's in your head for the rest of your life.

2
IF I CAN DO IT SO CAN YOU

I remember the first time someone bought an expensive info product from me...

It. Was. Crazy.

I remember telling my buddy, "Someone just paid me **a thousand dollars** for something that *came out of my brain*." I was almost giddy. It was my first REAL foray into what has become a deep passion.

I sold what was in my head and someone actually wanted to buy it!

I hadn't used a shovel or punched a time-card. I hadn't reported for duty or signed in. I hadn't called a meeting. And yet, here was that glorious email staring back at me from the computer screen.

"Congrats Jake, You've Got A New Student In Your Class"

I was hooked. Game over.

It was on like donkey-kong from that point forward.

I appreciate my wife and kids for sticking with me through those first few months of infopreneurship. I nearly killed myself creating my first online course and then stressed like a maniac building a webinar, deadline funnel, autoresponder sequence, sales page, Facebook ads, and more!

It was honestly one of the hardest things I ever did.

I'll talk about it in more detail in a later chapter but let me just say this.

I'm SO glad you've got this book in your hands because it's going to save you *a lot* of time, stress, and money!

But, I don't regret the struggle I went through because it brought me to the place I am now. I'm an infopreneur. I create knowledge based products and sell them on the internet.

It's a pretty cool place to be.

The other day I woke up and saw that I'd made $1200 while I slept. And, I had an email in my inbox from a student *thanking me* for creating the course. How cool is that?

As my three year old daughter says, *"Are you joking me?"*

Later that same day I took a nap (I promise I don't just sleep all the time...haha) and when I woke up...another $1200.

Making $2400 in one day while you nap ain't too shabby…

Now, before you get *too* excited, you need to know that I'd put in a TON of effort and energy to get to the stage of making money while I slept.

It wasn't easy. But the reward is sweet.

And even though it was a lot of work it didn't require a huge financial investment or complex business model.

It was a class on church outreach that I recorded on a $50 webcam in my home office. I didn't have an email list. I didn't have a following on social media. I didn't have thousands of dollars to spend on Facebook ads.

What I had was a little bit of know-how and a whole lot of determination.

I'd heard about people selling books, courses, software, and services for stupid amounts of money (stupid being good in this case...ugh, Millennials and their verbiage...am I right?) and I wondered if maybe I could do it too.

And guys, this wasn't in 2003...it was 2018. I didn't "get into the game" at the start. People had been making and selling info products way before me. It just goes to show that it doesn't matter when you start. The only limitation is you!

Now, let's talk turkey (whatever that means).

Not every day is a massive win as an infopreneur.

In fact, those days are kind of like the "one shot" you make in golf.

The putt you sink from 20 feet out. Or, the lucky 9-iron that lands "just right" on the green.

Those shots (and days) are the ones that keep you coming back.

It's probably a good time to deal with something important. So let's just get it out of the way now. If you think that selling what's in your head is an easy way to get rich quick or an excuse to be lazy you might as well check out now.

There's probably a St. Vinnys or Goodwill somewhere close to you where you can donate this book. This isn't a gimmick for me. It's a passion and a calling. We'll go into what that means in a later chapter.

What I'm going to teach you how to do isn't a "get rich quick scheme." It's a mindset, philosophy, and a process. It takes time, money, effort, commitment, and character. The bottom line for me isn't the *bottom line*. It's about creating value for my family *and* the world around me by using my God-given intellect to create mutually beneficial products and services.

I'm a firm believer that every business deal should end with at least two happy people. I serve my customers and they pay a fair price. We both walk away happy. That's the kind of business I run and the kind I teach.

If that sounds like your cup of tea then keep on reading.

It's going to get fun real fast!

But let me backtrack a bit…

Because I didn't start out selling high-ticket courses. It was a much more humble beginning.

My first deep-dive into **selling what was in my head** came on Amazon. I'd written a book about prayer and Bible reading for the youth group I served at. It was literally only twelve-thousand words long…really more of a long essay than a book! But, I found out about Amazon ads and started putting a few bucks a day on it.

To my surprise, real-life, *actual* humans started buying it! I was rich…well, err, not exactly. I think I sold 6 of my books on kindle for $3.99 on my very best day for a profit of about $15 after advertising. Nowhere near champagne wishes and caviar dreams…

But I was hooked.

I kept at it and ended up making $100 bucks a month using Amazon ads to sell my book. I was really excited because I'd sold a few dozen books in the years since I'd written it and now I was selling a book every day! Pretty cool.

At that point I realized I was onto something but I wasn't satisfied…

I was paying Amazon to advertise my book *and* a cut of every sale. At the end of all that I wasn't getting any customer info. Amazon was. And I was the one who'd done all the work writing the book!

Then the thought struck. What if I created a simple video course and sold it for $29 rather than an eBook for $3.99? What if I could get off Amazon's platform, stop paying them most of my profits, and start building relationships with my own customers?

At the same time, I also started learning about how important email lists were. Everyone said, "The money is in the list." I didn't even know what that meant at first. But after reading everything I could get my hands on, it started to make sense. A list is just a relationship with a lead or buyer. When someone opts in to your list they give you permission to communicate with them. And there's HUGE value in that which we'll go into later...

So, armed with a determination to increase my profits and build a list I recorded a 4 part video course (less than an hour long), designed a cover on Canva, and dove in with both feet. I put together what's called a "lead magnet" and offered it to people for signing up for my list. And after a month or so, I had 100 people on my email list!

But I really had no idea what to do with them. At the time I was deathly afraid to send them an email because they may *gasp* UNSUBSCRIBE! What I didn't know far outweighed what I did. Those early days were a whirlwind of trying to figure out the tech and the techniques I would need to be successful.

Honestly, it was tough. As you've probably found out, there's a LOT of information out there and usually someone trying to sell you something (which is more than fine but it makes it hard to know who to trust). But I pushed through the fear and started hacking through the jungle of uncertainty.

Which is what you'll have to do as well if you want to be successful. It's scary, I get it. You probably have a million questions. There are so many voices yelling at you to "do this" or "do that!" But don't worry. If you just keep hacking through that jungle...you'll make it. And it's totally worth it!

Several months into my journey I looked up and could see the blue sky in my business for the first time. People were joining my list. I was making sales and people were even emailing me saying they liked the course and how it was helping them! That's a truly great feeling.

And I want YOU to experience it too!

But before we move on, let's define what we're talking about.

"Selling what's in your head" refers to taking something you know, packaging it, presenting it, and selling it to someone else that wants to know it too. That's it!

This can be done in an almost infinite amount of ways.

• Books/eBooks

• Courses

• Coaching

• Consultations

• Workshops

• Masterminds

• Memberships

• Mentoring

• Checklists

• Worksheets

• Surveys

• Q&A's

• How To Guides

• Screen-shares

• Webinars

• Conferences

• And on and on it goes…

Information has always been productized and monetized (ahem...we're looking at you student loans!) but the internet and social media have turned a trickle into a torrent. As noted earlier, the global e-learning (electronic) industry will account for 275 BILLION dollars of commerce in the year 2022.

I don't know what side of the tracks you grew up on but to me that's A LOT of money. And what's fascinating is that the revenue generated from info products is almost pure profit. Information requires nearly no overhead. There are no warehouses or shelves to stock. No real estate. No need for endless armies of sales people.

In fact, solo-infopreneurs can often generate MILLIONS of dollars of business ALL BY THEMSELVES.

That gets me excited for a bunch of reasons but here's two:

• I'm impatient.

◦ I hate the idea of waiting on someone else to finish something before I can bring my ideas to life. Infopreneurship allows me to operate at the speed of thought.

• I'm independent.

◦ I don't want my financial or creative future in someone else's hands. I want to drive. I love working with a team but I know that I'm wired as a creative leader. I'm at my best when I can create, communicate, distribute, and serve.

That's why I love knowledge based business and why I am so passionate about helping you create an info product of your own.

And that's what you're going to do but first you need to learn the #1 secret of selling what's in your head.

3
THE #1 SECRET OF SELLING WHAT'S IN YOUR HEAD

The LEVERAGE Principle

It's called "leverage," and it's how you're going to achieve ALL of your goals by selling what's in your head. This is by far my FAVORITE part of being an info-preneur.

Let's break it down, shall we?

For our purposes, "leverage" refers to creating something once and then selling it again and again and…

It's such an incredible thing. You spend time and effort creating your info product ONCE but then you can just sit back and let it work for you FOREVER. Think about it. You're reading this book right now (an info product) and hopefully getting value out of it. I'm teaching you something. I'm *working*…but I'm not.

I'm probably hanging out with my kids or eating a hamburger while you read this. I did the work *once* but now this book is doing the work for me *again and again*.

That's leverage.

Remember when I told you about selling my online course while I slept?

That's leverage.

It's one of the main reasons this knowledge based business model is so great.

You work just as hard as anyone else but your work goes on working for you after you're done.

And, when they're digital, info products are infinitely reproducible and don't take up space in a warehouse or on a shelf. They don't go bad or become stale. And you can sell them again and again and never have *less*.

Pretty cool in my book.

Most people are stuck on the hamster wheel of trading time for money. You know exactly what I mean. Maybe you're trying to escape it...

It's the 9 to 5 grind.

That soul-crushing struggle for survival where you work really hard just to make ends meet and end up not really enjoying the result.

When you understand and use the "Leverage Principle" you can get off the hamster wheel and start enjoying your life.

You can work on things that are meaningful to you and that make the world a better place.

And break the "time for money" cycle once and for all.

Now, you need to understand something before we go on. There's really no such thing as "passive" income. Passive people are poor or work for "The Man." Passive income only comes from serious action! But if you're willing to work hard and be smart about what you work on you can use the leverage principle to create income producing products that work *for* you.

And, it's certainly not just about making money…

Many great teachers are stuck in the time for money continuum and are doing the world a disservice by not using a leveraged model.

They're depriving the world of their brilliance by limiting access to their knowledge. Why not share the wealth?

Maybe you say, *"Yeah, but isn't face to face instruction always better?"*

#1 - **Not Always** - Sometimes people learn better at their own pace and in their own environment. Many people actually prefer the lower pressure environment of remote learning. For others, their schedule or life situation makes it impossible to study or learn face to face. This is why books have always been and always will be a HUGELY popular and influential means of transmitting information and ideas. They're portable, transferable, scalable, and you can read on your own terms.

#2 - **Something Is Better Than Nothing** - If you have the opportunity to learn something in a limited capacity or not at all which is better? Yup. Something is better than nothing! In my personal business, there are definitely some disadvantages to coaching and strategizing remotely with my clients but the positives far outweigh the negatives. I get to help train people all over the world who otherwise wouldn't get to work with me. Something is better than nothing.

That's why I love info products. They're one of the absolute best ways to stop trading time for money and start using the "leverage principle" to help yourself and others.

An online course is a great example of leverage. You put the work in to learn and hopefully master a useful skill or knowledge set once and then *leverage* that information again and again through the online course. Once, the knowledge or skill is captured in a repeatable format (video, audio, written word) it can be leveraged again and again.

Of course, the most common form of leveraged info products throughout history have been books. Once they're written and produced they can go on nearly forever (especially if the information isn't time sensitive). But all kinds of products can be leveraged!

With the right leverage-able product you can build an entire business (I did…) and help tons of people in the process.

And that's what you should start envisioning right now.

- What information can you "leverage" and productize?

- What is something in your brain that other people might find valuable?

- What's a "BIG" problem you've solved? It doesn't have to be unique…just valuable, e.g., you know how to change a transmission without taking your car to the mechanic.

- What would be the easiest and fastest way to transfer this knowledge? A book? A list? A video?

Don't worry if you don't have any killer ideas right off the bat. And don't go too deep just yet.

The goal is to start exercising your creative thinking muscle with leverage as the goal. Because once you do it gets exciting. The possibilities are nearly endless.

Here's a pro-tip:

When you're getting started **your biggest enemies are fear and overwhelm.**

It's incredibly hard to wade through ALL the options and possibilities, especially when you still don't know *what* to do or *how* to do it. But don't worry. By the end of this book you'll be equipped with what you need to know to create and launch your first leveraged info product.

But to make it more simple, limit your thinking to creating an eBook or simple online course. These are proven info product models and they're fairly easy to create.

Now I know the idea of "writing a book" might freak you out but that's not what I'm talking about.

When I say (eBook) I'm talking about a simple document that you can create in a single afternoon. Something that solves one problem or teaches a skill…

It doesn't have to be (and shouldn't be) complex or exhaustive.

Some info product ideas to get you started:

1) A simple eBook (PDF) that solves a big problem or teaches a skill, e.g.,

- "How to catch BIGGER fish than your friends using THIS casting trick!"
- "5 Ways to Maximise Your Tax Refund This Year"
- "How To Get An Extra Hour Of Sleep Per Night"
- "6 Master Dog-Training Secrets That Beginners Can Use"

2) A simple video-course doing the same thing as above (solving a problem or teaching a skill.)

- "Fear Factor: 3 Techniques To Overcome Speech Anxiety"
- "The Five Things You Need To Know To Crush Your Next Job Interview"
- "How To Apply Eye-Shadow Like A Pro"

As you can see from the examples above, it can be simple.

People successfully sell eBooks (or physical books) on ALL kinds of topics for $20-$500!

And online courses can and do sell for $50-$5000 depending on the market and offer.

But for now, just focus on the "Leverage Principle."

You're going to create something once and sell it again and again (cool right?) but not just yet.

Because there's definitely a "right" way and a "wrong" way to approach this, especially when you're just getting started, and I want to help you succeed as quickly and painlessly as possible.

Read on.

4
THE ONLY THINGS THAT MATTER

Now that we've laid the foundation it's high-time you learned how to launch and run your own info-product business.

So I'm shoving you out of this comfy nest little bird!

Here are your *"on the way down"* flight tips.

You need to know that **most people overthink and overcomplicate business**...especially online info-product businesses.

But you're not going to do that…

As long as you understand that...

All business boils down to three things:

1. Something to sell.

2. Someone to sell it to.

3. A way to sell it.

You need a market, an offer, and a process.

That's it.

Drill those three things into your brain.

Say them out loud a few times. Seriously…say them out loud.

"Sir yes sir! Something to sell, someone to sell it to, and a way to sell it! Market, Offer, Process!"

You can now safely ignore 99% of the complex crap being taught "out there."

Most of it doesn't matter…

These three things are the only things that matter. They will determine your success or lead to your failure.

Market - Offer - Process

You're now in the "MOP" business and you're here to stay.

Here's my first "MOP" - how I literally built a multiple six-figure business in less than a year…

Market: Pastors and church leaders (that want their churches to grow but don't know how to make it happen)

Offer: Church Marketing Masterclass (Online course teaching them how to grow their church)

Process: FB Ad to Webinar to Sales Page to Email Follow-Up

Yes, there are some additional technical bits and pieces in the distribution chain (course hosting, online cart, etc) but the fundamentals are simple.

Here's another one I've done successfully.

Market: Pastors and church leaders (that want their churches to grow…yes the exact same market…*why mess with success right?*)

Offer: Facebook Invitation System (Online course teaching them how to make simple Facebook ads to grow their church…yes pretty much the same offer as before but a variation on it and a lower price)

Process: FB Ad to Sales Page (dead simple…)

Both of the examples above produced six-figure or higher revenue streams and continue to be viable to this day…

And here's one more in a different niche.

Market: eCom store owners (that want to grow their business with info products)

Offer: Sell What's In Your Head (Book, online course, and community)

Process: Ad to Opt-In to Sales Page

Something to sell, someone to sell it to, a way to sell it.

All you need is a M.O.P.

And to really do it right and be successful you'll need to build your MOP sequentially…

But the process is fairly simple and straightforward.

#1 Choose a "hot" market. (I'll explain this in a later chapter.)

#2 Create an offer the market REALLY wants.

(With your info product at the center of course.)

#3 Drive traffic to a page that sells it.

So, let's talk about each of these steps in more detail starting with your market…

5
MARKET FIRST

This chapter is worth its weight in gold. And it will save you a TON of time, money, and frustration.

Whether you're experienced or not you need to read this. Because there's nothing that will impact your success and potential sales more than your market. **If you choose the right market, sales will almost make themselves!** But if you choose wrong...it will be much more difficult.

First, what is a market?

Here's a definition from netmba.com,

"In marketing, the term market refers to the group of consumers or organizations that is interested in the product, has the resources to purchase the product, and is permitted by law and other regulations to acquire the product."

That one is fine but here's my dead-simple definition:

A market is a group of people that share a problem or desire.

Here's an example: **dog owners.**

What are some potential problems they might have?

- Cleaning up dog poo (hated this when we owned dogs… this problem stinks)
- Barking (the neighbor is mad and your wife is DONE with Fido…)
- How to train their dog ("Sit, no I said SIT!")
- Biting ("He's really the *sweetest* dog…")
- Doggie health (Vet bills anyone?)

Those are off the top of my head and I don't even own a dog right now. I'm sure you could find a hundred other problems or sub-problems that need solving.

And every single one of those problems is something someone would pay you to solve…or teach them to solve. And the good news is, the easier and faster you can provide that solution…the better.

Here's what you need to know.

Your market determines the floor and ceiling of your business. The floor is the baseline income you can make. The ceiling is the cap or potential of profitability.

It's really just common sense. If your market is HUGE and HUNGRY it's easier to sell more and faster. If your market is small and satisfied there are less available buyers.

Now, like everything there are exceptions to the rule.

There's a saying that goes: *The riches are in the niches.* And this is true when your niche is in a hot market.

Because there's money in every market (I heard of a person making 7 figures a year in the knitting market, go figure!)…but I highly advise picking a hot market.

A hot market has three factors:

Passion, Money, and Momentum.

And you can use the "P.M.M. Formula" to help guide you to the right market.

Passion = Does it stir emotion? People care about this. It has the ability to make them sad, happy, or angry. *Politics anyone?*

Money = Do they have it and are they willing to spend it to solve their problem?

Momentum = Is the market in motion? Are they already running around frantically trying to find a solution?

In my opinion a market needs to score 2 or more on the P.M.M. scale to be worth your time but I definitely recommend going for a market with all three.

This is what Ken McCarthy (called the father of internet marketing) says about it,

> *"The 'WHO' is the market you choose to sell to. And here's the rest of 'the secret'...*
>
> *'Some markets are hard and some markets are easy'. If you want to make maximum money in minimum time go after 'easy' markets.*
>
> *What do I mean by an 'easy' market? 'Easy' markets have the following three characteristics.*
>
> *They are:*
>
> *1) Easy to reach*
>
> *2) Have a burning 'need' for what you've got, and*
>
> *3) Have demonstrated through past behavior an ability and willingness to spend money on the kinds of things you plan to sell*
>
> *The closer the market you choose corresponds to this description, the easier your marketing life will be."*

Historically, there are three BIG HOT markets. Health, Wealth, and Romance.

Everyone wants to be healthy, rich, and find love (or lust...but that's another discussion). So, if you can choose a market that fits into one of these three you'll do fine.

Practically, you need to choose a market or sub-market to serve. The reason this comes before a product or offer is because you'll create your product based on what the market already wants...**which practically guarantees it will sell!**

Please don't overthink this. If it's your first go round you'll probably make mistakes. But that's OK. Because even if you don't hit the bullseye on your first try you'll get close enough if you use the "P.M.M. Formula" I just taught you.

Another factor in choosing a market is taking stock of what you know or have *any level* of expertise with.

Let's say you decide on the health market and your niche is young moms who are *fed up* with dieting (see what I did there?). You've got a great idea to help them lose weight without giving up pizza or chocolate because **that's what you did.** That'll work just fine.

Anytime you can say, "Here's what I did to get X result" and it fits within a hot market, you've got the makings of a profitable idea.

Here's another one. It doesn't even have to be your idea or story. I'm an affiliate for several products/companies that solve problems in my market. And I can say, "Here's how they did it...or...here's what this did for me" and it works the same.

So how do you go about finding a market?

Allow sensei Ben Settle to drop some wisdom on you...

> "When the vast majority of people go into business and try to sell something, they almost always spend a lot of their time and money trying to find customers for what they have to sell.
>
> And if you ask 9 out of 10 business owners about this, they will

likely tell you this is exactly what they did—thought of a product idea then decided to start a business.

But here's the thing:

Those exact same people would have cut the time it took to make a profit in half if they'd simply did it backwards and found out what their leads/prospects already wanted first and then sold it to them."

In plain Jane english...

Choose a market *first*.

Don't start with an idea and then look for a group of people to sell it to. That's a good way to go broke.

At best you'll get lucky. At worst you'll make no sales.

And that's more like gambling rather than serious business.

So how do you find a red-hot buyer's market?

1. *Guess?*
2. *Ask people what they want to buy?*

Nope and nope.

Guessing definitely won't work...that's what you'd be doing if you just created and launched your product. Taking a shot in the dark.

So, what about asking your market?

First, it's almost impossible to do...doing a proper survey of a market takes a lot of time and money which you probably don't have if you're just starting out...and you definitely don't want to spend even if you're not...

The second reason asking your market doesn't work is because everyone lies.

"What Jake, are you serious?"

Bear with me. I'm not saying people intentionally lie but it's a well known phenomenon that we all want to appear better than we really are.

Perhaps a better way to put it is that we're all "aspirational."

We want to be a better version of ourselves so we tend to "project" an inaccurate picture when we're asked what we do or what we want.

Here's how this works in practice:

Say you ask your market, "Would you rather eat a candy bar or a carrot?"

A lot of people are going to say, "Carrot."

But those same people are going to stop at the corner store on their way home and buy a Snickers! Plus a bag of chips for later…

Because they *want* to be a healthier person that makes better food choices than they actually are. And they want *you* to think of them like that as well.

That's why asking a market isn't the best strategy to determine what products or offers to sell.

Here's what is.

Find out what your market is *already* buying and then sell them more of the same.

Example: If you're in the health niche and you see people breaking down the doors for Keto or low-carb diets…figure out a way to "repackage" or "align" with what they're already buying and offer them that.

You don't have to copy someone else. Just figure out how to carve a space out for yourself by differentiating *ever so slightly*…

This simple little tweak will make everything work better in your business.

It removes all the guesswork and makes it possible for you to create extremely desirable products and offers that are almost guaranteed to make your market go crazy for them.

This also levels the playing field for marketers and business people. Because it's not who writes the best ad copy or who has the best funnel that wins the prize. It's the person who knows the market best. *

And that my friend is how it's done.

Let's Recap:

- Before you create a product or offer choose a market.
- Study it and see what they're *already* buying.
- What are they passionate and excited about?
- What do they get emotional about?
- Does it align with something *you* know or are passionate about?
- Only after you've thought through and answered these questions should you try and create an offer for this market. Then, and only then, can you create irresistible products and make an offer they can't refuse…

Which is what we'll cover in the next few chapters…so read on my fine-feathered friend…

* *See appendix 2 at the end of the book about market research to get some practical ideas on how to do this.*

6
PRODUCT PALOOZA

Product creation is where most people freeze like a deer in the headlights when it comes to making money online.

Which is crazy because once you're done with this book you'll have more ideas than you know what to do with for how to create profitable products.

Once you've identified a market to serve and a problem to solve it's time to create a product to sell.

There are millions of potential products but for now we'll focus on info-products because they're quick to create and have incredible profit margins.

Info products come in all shapes and sizes: books, courses, workshops, live presentations, recordings, interviews, checklists, videos, audio, and on and on it goes.

Bottom line: An info product is information that has been created, curated, or designed with the intention of being sold. The form it takes, whether written, audio, or video is simply the delivery mechanism.

So, people ask me all the time, "What's the best thing to make? A course or a book? Or what?" And the answer is simply this: **What do you enjoy creating and what's best for the customer?**

Technically, I could teach the content you're reading via video or audio but I've chosen this medium (a book) for my own undisclosed nefarious purposes…

Actually, I'm happy to tell you because the villain always monologues, right? But not right now. I'll throw it in the back of the book and you can check it out later. Seriously, don't peek yet…

OK, I see you're back from reading the appendix now. So, let's keep going.

I recommend that you create a digital info-product if this is your first product. Digital products have the highest profit margin because there's no physical component costing you money to ship or store. Plus, you can add physical products to your lineup later.

But for now, focus on creating a simple (but high quality) digital product. Narrowing it down even further…make a mini-course (2 hours or less) or eBook that solves one of your market's problems or helps them achieve something useful.

The 10x Rule

Before we move on, let's get one thing straight. The world doesn't need another worthless product (info or otherwise). The internet is FULL of useless pdfs, guides, checklists, etc. So don't contribute to the problem. Be part of the solution. Create something that you're proud to put your name on.

Here's my litmus test: *Would I sell this to my own mother?*

Now, I can hear some of you smirking at that. I get that your mom probably isn't in your market. But if she was…would you feel good about her purchasing your product at the price you're offering? This brings us back to the 10x rule.

Ask yourself: *Is this product worth 10x what I'm asking for it?*

This advice goes directly against what almost every online goo-roo is currently teaching. They're saying *schtuff* like, "Just bust it out. You don't need to be an expert! Anyone can do it!" This is a short term mentality that leads to a short term business.

But that's not what I teach or believe in.

Sure, you can churn out "hype" info-products and convince people to buy them. But just so you know, the kind of people that are most likely to purchase these types of "hype-heavy" products are also the ones that are quick to refund and probably can't afford them in the first place...

So, long term, if you want to find fulfillment in your business dealings I strongly recommend avoiding this strategy.

But there's *another* reason why you should always put your best effort and energy into your products and offers. It's much more *profitable* in the long run.

Always, consider the long game. Because from the first minute you go public with a product or offer you're creating a perception in the minds of your market. And that perception is your *real* brand. Not your fancy graphics or logo. And not your cute mission statement...

Think about the term *brand* for a minute. It harkens back to the days of cattle-ranching. The *brand* was applied to the livestock to mark them as the property of a particular owner. A painful and permanent marking!

And that painful, permanent mark is being applied to your market's perception of *you* every time they see or hear from you. This is why you should never trade short term gains for long term ones. Never put the purchase above the person. When it comes to your products...think about the person on the other end.

If you treat them well they will reward you handsomely over and over again.

Consider the words of the late, great Earl Nightingale about who your *real* boss is,

> "So let's talk about you and your boss. Who is your boss? You have only one and every working person, from the president of the largest corporation to the shoeshine boy, has the same boss. **He is simply the customer.** There never has been, there is not now, and there never will be any boss but the customer. He is the one boss you must please. Everything you own he has paid for. He buys your home, your cars, your clothes. He pays for your vacations and puts your children through school. He pays your doctor bills and writes every paycheck you will ever receive. He will give you every promotion you will ever obtain during your lifetime, and he will discharge you if you displease him."

Mr. Nightingale is onto something there. The customer is your boss and he or she is the one you need to put first. If you follow this principle you'll never go wrong. At worst, you'll create better products and have the satisfaction of a job well done. At best, you'll be rewarded commensurately for your efforts. And my experience has been the latter. The "boss" pays well when you do your job with excellence.

Putting your blood sweat and tears into your products will ultimately pay off for you because it will also differentiate you from your competitors that take shortcuts!

As the legendary Warren Buffet quipped, "Only when the tide goes out do you discover who's been swimming naked." If your competition cuts corners and turns out inferior products, the market will eventually catch on. And, if you're doing quality work they will also catch on and spend their money accordingly.

Of course, marketing and advertising plays a big factor because the best product doesn't always win if nobody knows it exists. But that comes second to having a great product.

Now let's be clear on something.

When I talk about creating high quality products that doesn't mean they have to be big or long. In fact, it often means shorter and smaller...

It's about quality, not quantity.

And sometimes the 10x rule is honored by providing bonuses and additional content rather than through the product itself. But we'll talk about that later when we discuss making an offer your customer can't refuse...

Now that we've cleared that up, let's talk about how to create awesome info-products that help people and fly off the shelves.

Creating Your Product

As I mentioned earlier, your product could be any one of the following things:

- Book/eBook
- Course
- Coaching
- Consultation
- Workshop
- Mastermind
- Membership
- Mentoring
- Checklist
- Worksheet
- Survey
- Q&A's
- How To Guide
- Screen-share
- Webinar
- Conference
- And on and on it goes...

But let's focus in a little more.

I recommend a simple **online course** for your first product.

Here's why:

- **Leverage** - You create it once but you can sell it again and again. No more trading time for money.
- **Focus** - Going through the process of organizing and delivering your content will give you a crystal clear focus in your messaging and marketing.
- **Perceived Value** - It's easier to sell at a higher price point. This allows you to get more cash in your business quicker than trying to sell $5 ebooks. **Pro-Tip:** *It's not that much harder to sell high-ticket than low-ticket. It's all about matching supply and demand. People will compare your offer to other offers of the same price. So, if you're selling a video course for $500 they're not going to compare it to a $13.99 book on Amazon. They'll compare it to similar level offerings. Don't forget this!*
- **Value vs Time** - You can "splinter" off individual lessons or modules to create lead magnets or "tripwire" products. Your "one-time" investment of time and energy can be repurposed for lots of things!

Read on to learn my "Hacker" Course Creation Method for your profiting pleasure…

7

THE "HACKER" COURSE CREATION METHOD

Here's how to create a great online course FAST without being on camera or needing expensive equipment.

My favorite way to make high-quality online courses is by creating a slideshow using Powerpoint, Google Slides, or Keynote that you then record while you teach.

Essentially, you get your content together, put it in slides, and then record yourself teaching the content as you scroll through the slides.

This is a proven and effective method that allows you to deliver your content professionally without needing expensive gear.

You can do it with a laptop and simple microphone.

And there's no pressure of teaching it live or worrying about mess ups because you can edit out mistakes later.

Here are the steps:

1. Create your course outline.

I recommend using this format:

- **Introduction**: Introduce yourself briefly then introduce the course and explain the goal and benefits of completion. Tell your students what they'll get if they finish and implement the training. Briefly explain what they'll learn in each module.
- **Modules:** If your content has topics or sub-categories that build on each other towards the main goal then break each one into modules. A module can be one or more videos but always condense as much as possible. I also recommend using the rule of three in each module. Essentially, you have one main point and three supporting points. This is a useful way to organize information.
- **Conclusion**: Recap the one big idea of your course and the one big idea of each module. Tell them, "In module one you learned...in module two you learned...and on and on." Then remind them of the benefit of taking action on the information you gave them.

K.I.S.S. "Keep it simple sweetheart!"

Always deliver information in the simplest way possible and try to break things into steps. Try to get your students to the destination in the shortest amount of time possible. Think of yourself like an airplane pilot. Your passengers just want to get to the destination as fast as possible! Remove non-essential information and "rabbit trails." If something doesn't help your student get to their goal, get rid of it.

Pro-Tip: If you have a lot of helpful information that doesn't quite fit in your course, make a separate document or folder and use it as a bonus or even another course! *2 for the price of 1...pretty sweet!*

2. Create your slides.

I like Keynote - but you can use Power Point or Google Slides.

Make them clear. There's nothing wrong with black text on a white background. Don't use complex images or backgrounds. This will distract your students and bother some people.

Use Titles and Bullets. You don't have to write out every word of your course.

3. Record a voice-over as you go through the slides.

Keynote and Powerpoint let you do this but I don't believe Google Slides does at this time.

For the voiceover I recommend using a nice microphone rather than your built-in one. The Blue Yeti is a good option that a lot of people use.

4. Export the video.

Once you've recorded your voiceover on the presentation you can export it as a video. Make sure and name the file clearly so you can organize it later.

5. Export the slides as a PDF.

This gives your student a perfect "study-guide" and adds value to the course!

6. (optional) Extract the audio from the video.

Some of your students would rather learn via audio (like me!). If you include the audio files of the course it significantly increases the value of your product. Or, you can sell it as an upgrade if you want. But this gives you options.

There are several FREE services you can find on Google that will extract audio from video and create an MP3.

7. Choose a delivery method.

I've used a bunch of different methods but I currently do one of two things.

- **Use Kajabi:** Kajabi is an online course hosting platform that allows you to upload your video, audio, and notes into a secure platform where your customers login to consume it. They also have a mobile app that your students can use to access your content on the go. It's extremely nice and professional looking. But, it does cost around $120 per month. You can get a FREE 28 trial by using my partner link at: www.boringoldbusiness.com/tools
- **Use Samcart:** For those on a tighter budget you can still deliver your online course by putting the content into a folder on your computer and then sending people the folder when they purchase. Be aware that you'll have no control of the content once you send it this way. So piracy is a concern. But if you're selling a course under $300 I wouldn't worry too much about it. Samcart is my favorite software for this method because it will automatically deliver files up to 1gb for FREE when someone makes a purchase. This allows you to compress your course folder and have it delivered to your customers. You can sign up for their best deal using my partner link at - www.boringoldbusiness.com/tools

To access the best deals on the software tools just go to:

www.boringoldbusiness.com/tools

* To learn the "Hacker" sales method that you can use to market and sell your courses FAST see the appendix at the back of the book.

8
THE "HACKER" EBOOK CREATION METHOD

Simple eBooks are another of my favorite info products to create...

Want to learn how to create simple eBooks in just a few days that you can sell for a tidy profit?

Read on.

The first thing you need to understand is that you're not "writing a book" in the traditional sense. Sure, you can do that but it has some big downsides.

If you go on Amazon you'll see that prices are tightly controlled and 99% of books are sold for around $10. The book "market" has been shaped by powerful corporate forces and is based on outdated pricing structures.

But you don't have to play that game.

If you think about it...there's no reason books should be priced uniformly. Why should a book about teenage dragon riders be priced the same as a book like the one you're reading that's teaching you how to create a lifetime business?

Therefore, when you "free" yourself from the limited book publishing model you can break the rules that others are blindly following...

And that's exactly what you should do,

When you have valuable information to share you can charge what you want and if you can establish that value in the mind of your prospect they'll gladly pay it.

Another big myth about books is that the price is somehow connected to the length or size of the book.

Again, think about how crazy that is.

If you have a problem and I can solve it faster than the guy down the street wouldn't you rather save the time and work with me?

And that's how we think about value when it comes to time/length/etc in all kinds of markets.

People pay more for the mechanic that provides quality service *faster*. In the same way, a *shorter* book that gets you where you need to go can actually be positioned as *more* valuable.

Furthermore, most non-fiction books are filled with "fluff" that doesn't actually help you accomplish your goals.

If you get rid of the "fluff" and just teach the thing it's actually easier to sell it.

With all that being said, here's how to do it.

- Choose a "hot" market.
- Identify a problem they have.
- Solve it for them. (e.g., busy businessmen that want to get in shape but still want to eat candy bars.) Do you have a solution? Can you create one? The bigger the problem and the more your market wants it solved the better...
- Create a step by step outline.
- Write a chapter on each step...something like...

- Step #1
- Step #2
- Step #3

- If you can solve a "big" problem for someone and deliver that solution in a short book they can consume in one sitting they'll be happy!
- And that's something you can price accordingly.

For the actual writing, editing, formatting, and production of your eBook here's what I recommend.

First create your outline.

This will save you time and frustration down the road.

Write down your topic or "big idea" for the eBook.

What problem are you solving or what are you teaching?

It should answer this question: "What's the ONE thing I want my reader to walk away with?"

Once you know the answer to that question just teach them the steps or information they need to get to that goal.

Then use Google Docs and create a folder named for your book title.

Create a new document for each section and chapter, e.g., Intro, Chapter 1, Chapter 2, Chapter 3, Conclusion, etc

Write it!

Writing

It may seem daunting to "write a book" but put that out of your head. You don't need to worry about how long it is or how many words or pages it ends up being. Just worry about communicating the "one thing" or "big idea" to your reader as best you can.

Don't edit yourself as you write. Just let the words flow out naturally. If you have stories, tell them! Examples, use them!

You can edit it all later. But the main thing is just getting words onto paper.

If it's not something you can write in one-sitting, which most of the time it won't be, then you'll need to set aside time to write every day.

Here's what I recommend.

Identify the time of day you're at your best, e.g., early morning, afternoon, or late night. Then, carve out an hour to write your eBook. Take this time seriously! You're creating an "asset" for your business that you'll be able to make money from for the rest of your life.

If you write for one hour a day until it's done you'll knock it out faster than you could ever imagine. Don't underestimate the power of consistency.

And, once you get your first one done…it will be that much easier to do another and another…

Once you're finished writing it's time to edit, format, and produce your book.

Editing

For editing, use the spellcheck in Google docs first.

Then read through your book quickly and find any "wooden" passages that may need to be re-written. Does it sound natural when you read it out loud? If not, just quickly change it.

Do this natural read-through a few times until you're confident your book "sounds like you" and flows.

Be aware that perfect grammar, spelling, etc is far less important than the "feel" of your book. If the information is great and it flows

I'm happy as a reader! Perfect grammar and spelling in a book that doesn't flow is a no-no.

If you're really concerned with editing have a "grammar nazi" friend do a read through for you. Buy them pizza for their time! That's a non-negotiable.

Even better have two different people do a read-through. You'll be surprised how each one finds different things that require editing.

Formatting

For formatting you're in luck. This used to be a HUGE chore or expense but now there are some incredible FREE or inexpensive options available.

My first recommendation is to use https://reedsy.com/write-a-book

Reedsy is a website for writers and they have a variety of services you can use but they provide a free book formatting tool at the link above. I've used it several times and it's great!

Not only will you get a PDF but you also get popular eBook formats that you can provide to your customers.

Another option for formatting is to use someone on fiverr.com that does book formatting. But only do this AFTER you've tried Reedsy's book formatting tool. Fiverr is a mixed bag and results vary depending upon who you hire.

One last formatting idea is to use a design tool like Canva to create a PDF if your book is short. This is the most time consuming and technical option but you can create really nice looking designs with it.

If your book has a lot of pictures or graphics you'll probably want to hire a formatter or use a professional tool.

But I recommend keeping it simple for your first try at least.

Cover Design

For your ebook cover you have a few options.

- Hire a designer
- Do it yourself
- Use a template

You can hire a designer on fiverr or other book cover websites but I don't recommend that unless you already have a big customer base waiting to buy your book.

Another thing you can do is design it yourself in photoshop or other design software...

But, why make it harder than it needs to be?

I recommend you use a template from a design tool like Canva or Snappa. You can use one of their templates as a starting point.

Choose a book cover template you like and then change the colors and maybe the font but don't try to be Picasso...just keep it simple. The template was professionally designed and it works! So don't overthink it...

Then upload the finished image into Reedsy where it will be added to your formatted book and...

Badda bing badda bang...you've got yourself a PRODUCT to sell!

The most basic format you'll need is a PDF. And you can do just fine selling ONLY that.

This is the best and most important format because it's easy to distribute and almost everyone has a way to read it.

Pricing

Let's talk about pricing for a minute.

And this will apply to all your info products and business strategies.

I almost never recommend selling "cheap" products.

Sure, you might make a few more sales up front but you'll attract the wrong type of person and ultimately devalue your brand.

You've got to keep in mind that with info products you're selling a skill or a solution to a problem. So what's that result worth?

You're not selling the value of the bytes or the paper…

You're not selling your time…

You're selling the RESULT.

And you should price your products accordingly and then explain that clearly.

Take the book you're reading right now for example.

The reason I priced it the way I did is because the RESULT I'm offering is *incredibly* valuable!

It's worth far-more than the paper and ink, digital storage space, bytes, 1's and 0's ets that it requires to deliver.

So don't price your products based on the mechanism. Price them based on the result.

9
CREATING A "NO-BRAINER" OFFER

After you've chosen a market to serve and decided on a product you'll need to craft an offer.

And I want to to teach you how to make: **"No-Brainer Offers!"**

Because *creating* products is the EASY part.

But *selling* products is a whole different animal...

And there's a secret to creating products that people will actually buy.

Sure, you *could* just slap a picture of your product with a "buy now" button on a website and hope for the best...or you can learn the art of the offer.

And I'll tell you right now, **the real money is in the offer.**

Very simply, an offer is saying: **"Here's everything you're going to get and what it's going to do for you if you buy…"**

An offer can be a single product, a product with bonuses, several products bundled together, or even a combination of products and services.

But a great offer should be almost irresistible to your target customer.

When you've done your market research correctly you should know almost everything your market wants…but also what they *crave*. You should know what drives them crazy and makes them burn with anger, what their dreams are and, what problem they would give almost *anything* to solve.

When you know these answers it's fairly easy to make a great offer.

Like the late, great Peter Drucker said,

> "The aim of marketing is to make selling superfluous. The aim of marketing is to know and understand the customer so well that the product or service fits him and sells itself."

- So, you know your market inside and out.
- You've created a product that you *know* they desperately want/need.
- Now comes making your offer a "no-brainer" for the customer to buy.

At this stage it's about **increasing the value of your offer** so that it's nearly a no-brainer for your customer to buy.

Here's a simple equation I use to create "no-brainer" offers:

"No-Brainer Offer" = perceived value > 10x cost.

A "no-brainer" offer is where the perceived value to the customer is at least ten times the price.

So if you're offering an eBook about fishing with 3 bonuses for $49 the customer should perceive it's value as $490. *Make sense?*

Let's put that in investment terms.

If I said to you, "Here's an investment where you put in $100 and in a month you're guaranteed to get back $1,000," would you do it?

You bet you would. A 10x ROI is insane…

Some might say a no-brainer!

And that's the level of value you want your customer to perceive in your offer. That's the 10x rule in a nutshell. Always provide 10x the value vs the cost. Obviously worth and value are relative but when you know how to explain value you'll see how this works.

The idea behind a "no-brainer" is for the customer to almost think, "This is too good to be true." And then, your job as the seller is make sure it's not!

In other words, you're actually going to deliver the goods the "no-brainer" offer promises. And in the process, turn your buyers into fanatically happy customers for life!

Ever seen an infomercial?

Sure they're cheesy but those people know how to sell!

And you know that part when they say, "But that's not all!"

It's exciting isn't it?

Because usually by that point you're usually ready to buy whatever it is they're selling…

But then they add a second product, then a bonus, then slash the price. It's awesome!

And they keep increasing the value until it feels like you'd be *losing* money if you didn't buy. That high-point is what you want to achieve with your offers.

So how's it done?

Lost Art of the "No-Brainer" Offer

As I mentioned before a true "no-brainer" offer will follow the 10x rule where the perceived value is at least ten times greater than the cost of the offer.

You want your offer to **feel like a great deal** to your customer.

Here's where most people mess it up.

They think **"great deal" = "low price."**

They hear that a "no-brainer" offer should feel like a great deal and think, "I've got to lower my prices!"

That's a HUGE mistake!

Oftentimes they get *less* sales and make *less* money when they do this.

Because pricing is always *relative* to perceived value.

A great deal doesn't automatically equal cheap or inexpensive.

Great deals are about perspective and positioning.

People talk about getting great "deals" on $500,000 houses or $100,000 cars.

That's a lot of money…

But it's all relative right?

Because when you purchase a house you compare it to other houses in the same area and price range.

And so it is with products…including your ebooks or courses.

So how do you sell MORE and for a HIGHER price while still giving your prospect the experience of getting a great deal?

Instead of *lowering the price* you should **raise the value of your offer**!

And I'll give you all the tools you need to do exactly that in the next two chapters…

10

THE "NO-BRAINER" OFFER TOOLKIT

In the last chapter I introduced the idea of a "no-brainer" offer that's almost irresistible to your ideal customer.

The big idea behind a "no-brainer" offer is raising the perceived value and there are several tools you can use to just that...

Here they are:

1. Positioning
2. Pricing
3. Proof
4. Benefits
5. Bonuses
6. Timing

Tools For Building "No-Brainer" Offers

Tool #1 - Positioning

Positioning is what makes someone pay twice as much for a Mercedes Benz or only want to use Apple products...

It's how you "position" your brand, offer, and products as unique and potentially superior to similar ones in the market.

Here's a simple definition from StrategicCFO.com:

> "What is market position? In marketing and business strategy, market position refers to the consumer's perception of a brand or product in relation to competing brands or products. Market positioning refers to the process of establishing the image or identity of a brand or product so that consumers perceive it in a certain way.
>
> For example, a car maker may position itself as a luxury status symbol. Whereas a battery maker may position its batteries as the most reliable and long-lasting. And a fast-food restaurant chain may position itself as a provider of cheap and quick standardized meals. A coffee company may position itself as a source of premium upscale coffee beverages. Then a retailer might position itself as a place to buy household necessities at low prices. And a computer company may position itself as offering hip, innovative, and use-friendly technology products."

Many people are worried about competitors in a certain market. I've heard so many would-be entrepreneurs say, "Someone's already done my idea..." and then give up. But the presence of similar offers and products in a market isn't a good reason to stay away or quit.

Quite the opposite! If other people are making sales that means there are buyers in the market.

You just need to establish your unique position in that marketplace by answering a simple question: *What makes my offer different?*

Then lean into that market position and use it to increase your value.

One of the most powerful motivating factors in the world is scarcity. It's used everywhere to motivate sales. At grocery stores, online sales, movie theaters, and more!

And you want to know what there's only one of in the entire world?

You.

So, when it comes to selling what's in *your* head you're the only game in town.

And you can use your story and unique perspective to position yourself in the market.

I firmly believe this "secret" could be the difference maker for you in the long term.

When you realize your only *real* competition is yourself you'll do great. For years I worried about other people in my market... worried about if they were making more sales, releasing better products, or grabbing up the market share.

Then at some point I caught on. As an info-product creator and educator I'm a unique brand. And even if I teach on the same topic I do it with my own personality and style.

Think about Harvard and Yale. I'm willing to bet a lot of the information they teach is exactly the same. I'm sure they both teach math, physics, business, and a whole host of other topics. So what?

For some people it's Harvard all day. For others it's Yale.

Ivy-league throw-down!

Smart business owners realize that a competitor in the market has the potential to actually increase the size of the market.

That's why McDonald's and Burger King build near each other if possible. The guy driving by may have been thinking about a salad but then…boom…BK! Boom Mickey D's…now he has a choice to make but he's thinking burger and fries…not kale. He may give his business to Burger King on Wednesday but he's probably giving it to McDonalds on Friday…

See how that works?

So back to positioning.

You can increase the value of your offer by positioning it as unique. Let your personality shine when you're writing or on video. Don't try to be like everyone else. Be different and you'll create your own position.

Another quick thought on this is the idea of luxury.

And there are examples of it all around us.

Why are people willing to spend twice as much money for a certain brand of shampoo or soap when there's a perfectly suitable generic option on the shelf right next to it?

If the point of a car is to get you safely from point A to point B, why do some people opt for cars that cost 4 or 5 times the price of the standard model?

Luxury.

And luxury is all about the *positioning* of the brand or product.

See how you can apply that to your offer to increase it's value?

But the primary way to use positioning is through communicating your offer correctly.

It's the story, value, and emotional hooks you "wrap" around your product.

Here's a quick example:

It's a crisp autumn day. The leaves are golden and slowly falling from the branches above as you stroll down the sidewalk. Suddenly, a nice looking wooden chair in the window of a quaint little shop catches your eye so you stroll in.

A salesperson approaches…

> "Hi there, I noticed you looking at that wooden rocking chair? It's $359 and we take credit cards."

Sound good?

Sure! If you need a chair…and you're really ready to buy…

You might step up to the plate and become a customer. It's a nice enough product and the price seems fair…

But let's try again…

> "Hi, there. Can I interest you in this Hardwood Heritage rocking chair? It's hand-cut mahogany, custom built right here in our shop by one of our master-craftsmen. It's guaranteed for life and we'll even deliver it right to your house free of charge. If there's ever a problem with it you just let us know and we'll fix or replace it. This is a chair for people that aren't interested in cheap-throwaway furniture. We have customers that have passed these chairs down to their kids and grandkids. It's a worthwhile investment that will provide lasting joy to you and your family for a lifetime."

Which one do you think increases sales?

If you said door number 2…you're right!

That's a well positioned offer!

The product is wrapped in story, value, and meaning that goes beyond the product itself.

There's a focus on benefits (what it's going to do for *you*) rather than mere features.

The product is "positioned" in a way that makes it nearly irresistible to the right customer. And that's why you dig so deep into finding and studying your market FIRST. So you'll know exactly *what* it is about your product that will appeal to your target market.

Tool #2 - Pricing

This is the most obvious one. Most of us are conditioned to believe that a low price is a great deal. But do you buy your electronics at the Dollar store? Probably not.

Because a low price can also be a tip off to low quality…

So, think long and hard before automatically lowering your prices.

You might be sending the wrong signal to your prospects.

How can you use pricing strategies effectively to turn your offer into a "no-brainer?"

First, use price positioning.

Price positioning is where you introduce one price and get it rooted in a prospects mind and then drop it down at some point in your selling process.

Here's an example you can see all over big-box or grocery stores.

Most retailers will have two prices listed on their products. The "retail" price and the "discounted" price. Just go to your local grocery store and you'll see this over and over again.

"This loaf of bread is normally $4.99 but your price is $3.99!"

"These batteries are $3.65 today but normally $4.89!"

Unless it's a "loss-leader" sale they're probably not losing money on that transaction. Usually the real price is closer to the "discount."

You can do the exact same thing with your info-products by establishing the regular price and then introducing a discounted price (but what you're actually happy to sell it for).

The one issue with this strategy is that we're all on to it aren't we?

No one is really fooled but it still works psychologically at a subconscious level as long as you don't make it ridiculous.

A more nuanced approach isn't just to say "here's the normal price" and "here's the special price" but rather to establish the value of the product throughout the selling process and only introduce the price "drop" towards the end.

This strategy is far superior in my opinion because typically your prospect has decided to purchase *before* the price drop is introduced and then gets a "WOW" feeling when they see what a great deal they're getting.

But this is something you can experiment with in your offers.

Another pricing strategy is to use comparative value.

Value is almost always comparative in nature.

We perceive something to be a "great deal" when we recognize the value in comparison to something else of similar value.

This is why real estate agents always look for "comps" in a neighborhood when they're selling or buying homes. They want to see what values are established in the market.

The thing about info-products is they're notoriously hard to get "comps" for.

How do you really put a price tag on information?

It can't really be measured by the quality of the delivery mechanism unless you're selling rare books or something like that...

Which makes establishing comparative value both a challenge *and* an opportunity.

It's great if you can attach a monetary, emotional, or personal value to your product through comparison.

Here's an example.

Let's say you're selling an eBook on how to get rid of back pain with simple stretching exercises.

Most people would look at books on Amazon and think, "People will only pay $10 for this book." Big mistake.

Because you've got an incredible opportunity for value comparison on your hands!

- What would surgery cost in time, pain, and money?
- What are the side-effects of long term medication?
- How about the cost of long term pain and trauma?
- Experiences you can't live with your family because of your pain?

In light of those comparisons do you think it would be crazy to charge $50 or even $100 for your book? Would that still follow the 10X rule? You bet it would!

And if you can communicate that comparative value you will raise the value of your offer exponentially.

The last pricing strategy we'll discuss here is running a sale.

"Sales" are a time tested strategy for getting people to buy quickly and in a hurry.

The principle of the sale is simple.

Drop the price and create a deadline.

That's all there is to it.

But you need to be aware that "sales" are a two-edged sword and they cut both ways.

Sure, you can create a rush of buyers by using a sale but if you do it often you'll condition your market to only buy when there's a sale.

So, use them sparingly and strategically!

My favorite way to use sales is when I'm launching a new product to my list or at major holidays so there's a reason for the sale.

But don't stop there because there are more tools to discover!

11
THE "NO-BRAINER" OFFER TOOLKIT CONTINUED

Tool #3 - Proof

Whenever it comes to selling your products you've got to know something.

When they're reading your sales message your prospect is always thinking, "*Yeah right.*"

He or she doesn't believe your bold claims or big promises. They've seen too many ads (tens of thousands) and been let down too many times. This is why words like FREE and NEW and SECRET don't have as much impact anymore.

So how do you combat this advertising fatigue?

Simple.

Prove what you're saying by adding research, stats, quotes, witnesses, testimonials, experts, or whatever else you can throw in to increase credibility and believability.

If you're selling hype this won't work…but you're not doing that, *right?*

Because your product is actually good you should be able to back up your claims with some proof and evidence.

Gary Bencivenga, who's been called "the world's greatest living copywriter" said,

> "Never make your claim bigger than your proof. And always join your claim and your proof at the hip in your headlines, so that you never trumpet one without the other.
>
> There is no more powerful nor consistent way to explode your response. Surround your claims with stronger, bolder proof and watch your response soar."

This guy knows what the heck he's talking about. So you should listen!

If you want to increase the value of your offer simply include "proof" whenever and wherever you can in your advertising.

You can use:

- Reviews
- Customer Testimonials
- Quotes (from experts or celebrities)
- Research or Studies
- Statistics (if they're accurate and verified)
- Industry reports
- Websites
- Newspapers and magazine articles
- Historical figures (Did they say or do something you can connect to your product?)
- Stories (Your own or someone else's that connects to your offer)
- Reverse Proof (When you say, "I'm not an expert but here's what I've found it can actually increase your credibility!")

Pro-Tip: "But what if I don't have any user testimonials?"

No problem. You can borrow credibility. Find a celebrity or expert that said something that supports your idea or product and add the quote.

Let's say you're selling a course about budgeting. Go find a Warren Buffet quote where he talks about the wisdom of budgeting or something like it and put it on your page. Don't twist their meaning, mis-quote, or misattribute. That will BACKFIRE. But if you simply and accurately quote the known expert it does wonders for adding credibility to your claims.

Tool #4 - Benefits

Here's another important selling lesson:

Always turn features into benefits.

Take a laptop for example:

It has a hard drive, RAM, and a video card.

Those are the features of the product.

Every laptop sales page lists the "specs" of the equipment. "This laptop has 8gb of RAM, a 128gb HD, etc…"

But those features aren't what sells the product.

It's the "benefits" of those features that make the difference.

The 128gb HD will allow you to store more pictures of your family and your favorite music and videos.

The extra RAM will make browsing the web faster and more enjoyable…

The beefed-up video card will allow you to play modern games and watch Netflix in 4k…

Those are the benefits of the features.

Features on their own require the customer to think too much.

By explaining the benefits you paint a picture for your customer of how your product will make their life better.

So back to info products…

If you're selling information you need to make sure and explain the benefits of the information not just the features. You've got to go beyond explaining "what" you're teaching and step into the "why."

An easy way to do this in sales copy is to list a feature and then add the words "so that" to it.

Here's an example:

- *"You'll learn our proven method for balancing your budget **so that** you'll never have more month than money again!"*

And a few more variations on the same idea:

- *"Discover the secret way to prepare broccoli so your kids will beg for it rather than feed it to the dog under the table…"*
- *"Learn the powerful "5-minute weight loss" trick used by Hollywood producers to help their stars look great on camera that you can use to "cheat" yourself into your bathing suit…"*

Those are examples of features being turned into benefits.

The exact wording isn't that important. The idea is to clearly and simply explain why the feature matters.

That's the power of a benefit. It massively increases the value of your offer and moves it closer to "no-brainer" territory.

Use this tip and profit!

Tool #5 - Bonuses

Another powerful tactic when it comes to making your offer a "no-brainer" is by increasing the value "perception" of your product by adding bonuses to it.

Everybody, and I mean EVERYBODY, loves a deal.

I don't care if you're Bill Gates or someone living under a bridge...

Getting a bargain or more than you pay for is a powerful incentive to buy.

So, that's where bonuses come in.

Bonuses massively increase the value of the offer.

And can actually be the main reason someone buys your product... just to get it.

Bonuses are additional "products, services, features, or benefits" you add to your core product. They round out your offer and make it a total package.

Out of all the things you can do to increase the value of your offer, bonuses are easily the most powerful.

Some examples of what you can include as bonuses are:

- eBooks (guides, how-to's, etc)
- Audio (interviews, courses, etc)
- Video (courses, training, interviews, walkthroughs, etc)
- Checklists
- Resource Guides
- Templates
- Cheatsheets
- Graphic or design elements (for some products this makes sense)
- Coaching or consulting
- A 15 minute Q&A session with you...
- Swipe files
- Discounts on future products or services

One of the best bonus strategies I've used is to "bundle" my low-ticket online courses and include them as bonuses with my higher-ticket offers.

When I was getting started selling a high-ticket ($1,000) course I offered a free coaching session to the first five people that registered. This is obviously something that's not scalable but it worked great.

Before you go crazy just remember that not all bonuses are created equal.

There's an art to adding bonuses that ratchet up the value of your offer rather than just add fluff.

Rule number one is to add bonuses that compliment or expand your product.

If you're selling an eBook about how to train your dog you could include a video about dog nutrition and exercise. Don't add a bonus about tropical fish. That's not going to add value to your offer. Keep your bonuses closely related to your core product.

When I'm building offers I think strategically about the bonuses and ask, "What would take this offer over the top?" Remember, we want to make it a "no-brainer" for the customer.

I recommend that you create or choose your bonuses *after* you've created your product so you can fill in any gaps that you may have missed with your core product.

One thing you can do is give your info product to a few trusted people and ask them to tear it apart. Ask them what it's missing or what they wished they would have learned. What questions did it leave them with?

Then, take their feedback and go create two or three awesome bonuses that address what they said was missing.

This will *round* out your offer and make it a true "no-brainer" for future customers.

One final piece of advice is don't "overcomplicate" your bonus content.

You want it to compliment your core product, not compete with it. And if your bonuses are too complicated they will confuse your prospect and can actually *kill* the sale if you're not careful.

More bonuses are better but only if they add value to the offer.

Tool #6 - Timing

The last tool we'll cover is timing.

In business, as in life, timing is everything. And there are several ways you can leverage timing to increase the value of your offer and make it a "no-brainer" for your customer.

The first lesson is to leverage the market conditions that are happening at a given moment.

Take 2008 for instance.

If you don't remember, there was a HUGE market crash and people were freaked out about the economy and money in general.

If you had an offer that provided a solution to that problem, like "how to save your house from foreclosure" at that time you could have made a fortune. And many savvy marketers did!

So, always watch the market and be aware of what's going in the world that you could potentially benefit from.

This works for existing offers you have and for new ones you create depending on if the "event" is big or long enough to justify your effort.

Just be aware that if your product depends on something happening at a specific time its shelf life will only last as long as those market conditions exist.

Back to the 2008 economic crisis. Once the economy improved, the offers that were specific to those conditions became mostly irrelevant.

The second lesson about timing is:

Always leverage the power of urgency.

And this one is *really* powerful.

When it comes to creating info products, what you're offering is education or knowledge your market wants. And the "offer" is the WHOLE package including any discounts and bonuses.

But it's not enough to simply present the information or tell them what you're going to teach them.

You also have to show them why they need it NOW.

Here's the reality.

You may have a perfect offer that's being presented to the perfect customer but that doesn't mean they're going to buy…

In fact, most people *won't* buy.

For most of us, buying stuff is inherently scary. Even if it's exactly what we need. So we often need a little "push" to get us over the hump.

And that "push" often comes in the form of urgency.

Now, we've all seen artificial urgency being used in sales before: "ONLY HOURS LEFT - BUY NOW BEFORE IT'S GONE FOREVER!!!"

Only to see the same "*sale*" happen the next week and the next week after that.

That kind of "fake" urgency only works once. Then it will bite you in the butt.

So don't do it.

If you use urgency it needs to be REAL.

Go ahead and do sales with a deadline but make sure it's a real deadline and there's a reason for the sale like a Holiday or product launch. And use it sparingly.

But there's an even more powerful form of urgency you can use all the time that won't annoy your prospects but will still give them that internal push to buy right away.

It's what I call *psychological urgency*.

Psychological urgency uses the deep market research you've done to uncover what your market fears and what they crave. *Remember?*

Let's use weight loss as an example. If you're selling a product on how to lose 10 pounds in a month why does your prospect need to purchase right now?

Why shouldn't they wait?

Because they're missing out on the result and every day they wait is another day they'll spend trapped in their pain and problem!

All you need to do to create psychological urgency is identify and agitate their pain while dangling the solution in front of their nose.

Psychological urgency taps into your prospect's natural fear of missing out or being left behind.

And this is incredibly powerful when you're able to demonstrate what they're *already* missing out on rather than forcing their hand with fake urgency.

One of my mentors in sales says it's more powerful to influence people to buy rather than persuade them.

And that's exactly what psychological urgency does.

Make the pain vivid in your prospect's mind and then push on it. Then make the solution your product offers crystal clear and dangle it in front of them!

You can do this with stories, bullet points, testimonials, and anything else that keeps poking the sweet spot.

Another way to create psychological urgency is to use curiosity.

One of the greatest copywriters that ever lived identified curiosity as the most powerful weapon in advertising.

And when you pair curiosity with pain/desire you have a perfect cocktail of psychological urgency.

A Complete "No-Brainer" Offer

I've just given you six incredibly effective tools for crafting a "no-brainer" offer. Now it's up to you to master your craft using these tools. And the only way to do that is to use them. Remember, in sales and advertising there are no rules. Only results.

So do what works. Use what I've given you but adapt and add to it as you work on your own offers. But these six tools are a great starting point:

1. Positioning
2. Pricing
3. Proof
4. Benefits
5. Bonuses
6. Timing

Combine and interchange them. See how they interact, but most of all…**use them!**

12

SIMPLE SELLING PROCESS PART ONE

Now that you've zeroed in on your market and have a solid product and a "no-brainer" offer it's time to develop your selling process.

You've got to answer a few questions:

- *How will my target audience find out about my offer?*
- *How will I capture their attention?*
- *How will I communicate my offer once I've got their attention?*
- *How will I sell the offer?*
- *How will I deliver the offer?*

Let's assume that your online course can really help people do X or Y.

You know it solves a major problem or life issue or helps them achieve a dream.

But, no one else knows that because they don't know even know you exist!

And even if they did, they probably don't care…

Sorry Charlie but that's just the way it is.

So, how do you solve this?

The answer is a selling **process**.

And it has three parts:

1. Traffic
2. Conversion
3. Fulfillment

- **Traffic** refers to the amount of people you can get to check out your offer. The more eyeballs the better!
- **Conversion** refers to the opt-in (capturing their email so you can follow-up) or the sale itself depending on your objective.
- **Fulfillment** refers to how you will deliver the product and serve the customer.

Your process needs to account for these three things.

So Easy A Caveman Could Do It

Let's pause for a brief minute and get clear on one thing.

The simpler you make this the better.

It sounds a little scary when we talk about "traffic, conversion, and fulfillment" but it's really simple.

Traffic = people clicking your instagram post *or* reading your blog *or* a Facebook ad…just getting people to check out your offer…

Conversion = A webpage that gets people to buy or opt-in.

Fulfillment = sending them an email with their login information and then asking them how they're doing a week later…

See how simple that is?

You don't need to be Steve Jobs or Jeff Bezos right away…

I saw one guy the other day selling a one-hour webinar for $99 right from Twitter!

When you clicked the link in his tweet it went to a few paragraphs explaining what he has and a buy button. Maybe 300 words on that page? Nothing fancy…

And the dude pulls in thousands per month that way.

So don't think you need some fancy-schmancy, multivariate, built by robots, sales funnel with 19 *if/then* protocols…

Just get people to check out your "thang" and call it a day!

The good news is you only need to implement a simple process to get started.

I've experimented with a BUNCH of them but this one's easy to get off the ground.

Not only is it the fastest and easiest to pull off but it's also incredibly effective.

Many online business owners have built 7 and 8 figure businesses with this strategy ALONE…

And Ken Mcarthy, the "father" of internet marketing said that is how the REAL money has been and still is made online…

Ready for it?

- Opt-In (squeeze page)
- Sales Page
- Email Follow-up

To easy or good to be true?

Nope. Just good old fashioned common sense at work. Because typically the SIMPLEST explanation is the right one, right Ockham?

Just build a list (preferably email) of qualified leads and make a "no-brainer" offer.

Here's what it looks like spelled out a bit more:

You send traffic (paid or organic) to a page that captures email addresses. This page typically offers a "bribe" of some kind in exchange for the email. Often called a *lead magnet*. (I've put together an appendix that teaches you the basics of this at the end of the book.)

Then, the prospect is taken to a "thank you page" or directly to a "sales page" where there's an offer that's in line with why they signed-up in the first place…

Those that buy right away become customers. Those that don't buy are added to your email follow up list. And those emails typically "warm" up or "nurture" the prospect and send them back to the sales page to buy.

That's it!

Now, of course, there are LOTS of variations on how this can be done but it all boils down to the simple elements of:

- Opt-In (squeeze page)
- Sales Page
- Email Follow-up

To help you execute this simple process I've expanded it ever so slightly to make it easier to see the moving parts and what it takes to pull off.

I call it the "5x5."

To make this work you'll need 5 things.

1. One ad - This is what you'll use to bring people to your squeeze page.

2. One opt-in or "squeeze" page - This is the page designed to capture emails.
3. One lead magnet - This is the "bribe" you'll use to get emails.
4. One sales page - This is where you'll sell your offer.
5. One email follow-up sequence - This is what you'll send people that don't purchase right away.

With this strategy I'm assuming you're starting from absolute ZERO.

No audience, no fame or notoriety, no email list, no experience, and maybe even no money!

That's where I started...

But even if you start at ZERO this process can work for you.

My entire business model is dead simple.

Advertise into your target market and generate leads.

Then educate and nurture those leads until they buy.

Once they buy sell them something else.

And make the whole experience as fun, exciting, and informative as possible!

Market to leads to purchasers to customers.

Here's something to aim for.

Ever heard the "1000 True Fans" idea?

I highly encourage you to check it out here:

https://kk.org/thetechnium/1000-true-fans/

It was first introduced by Kevin Kelly back in 2008, and you should read his essay, but here's the core idea.

If an artist or creator can attract 1,000 true fans that purchase $100 worth of product per year directly from the creator it equals a $100,000/year career. Not too shabby right?

The idea here is that you don't need to sell a million products to the masses.

You can make a great yearly income with only 1,000 true fans!

Obviously you can slice this anyway you want.

If you're selling a $500 course you only need to sell 200 in an entire year. Around 17 courses per month (one every other day). Totally doable with the *entire* internet at your disposal.

If you're selling a $20 eBook you'll obviously need to sell a lot more!

But what if you have a few eBooks and courses? Repeat customers? A membership or continuity program of some kind with paying subscribers?

Only 1,000 true fans paying $100 per year.

What an elegant and reachable goal to aim for.

Getting excited?

You should…and I'm living proof that if you're willing to work hard and not give up you can get there even if you're starting from scratch!

Here's what I've done…

- Run FB ads offering a lead magnet. (Started at only $20 per day initially…)
- When people opt-in they're on my list where I send them a 5-7 day sequence of prewritten emails that tells my story and leads to an offer.
- Those that go through the welcome sequence without purchasing go onto my daily broadcast list.
- On the broadcast list I tell stories, share content, challenge

existing ideas, inspire, and provide opportunities to purchase my offers.
- Once someone buys they're on my buyers list and I make an offer for my membership or other products so they become a customer.

Here's the progression I'm after:

Market to **Lead** to **Buyer** to **Customer**

That customer level is similar to what Kevin Kelly calls a "true fan" who will typically spend $100 or more per year with my business.

Obviously, you've got to factor in business overhead and advertising costs. But this simple business model is proven and can work in any niche.

So what selling process will you use?

Your simple selling process just needs to deal with traffic, conversions, and fulfillment.

Once you figure out those three items you're off to the races.

13

SIMPLE SELLING PROCESS PART TWO

Now, I realize I just spent a whole chapter telling you how to go build a list with a lead magnet and then sell them something but I've recently discovered an even *easier, faster* and most importantly *more* profitable way to do it!

I call it the "Hacker Method" and it's laid out in detail in an appendix at the back of the book.

But here it is in a nutshell:

Instead of driving traffic to a squeeze page where you collect emails. You run an ad that sends people directly to a sales page where they purchase your product.

Catch that?

Instead of messing around collecting emails you just go straight for buyers…

For info products it usually works best to sell something less than $50 if you're advertising to "cold" traffic. Cold traffic means people that aren't familiar with you, your brand, or your product.

Now, a lot of marketers make a big deal about having to "warm" people up with free content and complex funnels where you only make an offer 19 years after someone signs up for your list…

But I've found that if you're advertising is clear, you have a "no-brainer" offer, and you know how to write a great sales page you can make a lot of sales.

This is a good time to mention that a lot of what's taught "out there" is overcomplicated B.S. because the "teacher" has something they need you to believe so you'll buy "their" secret system or process…

Bottom line: Hot market + Great Offer + Good Sales Page = Sales

Don't forget that equation!

And don't overcomplicate things. Set your goal and try to get there as quickly as possible!

If you're able to go directly from a FB ad to a sales page and make sales…why wouldn't you?

This is why I run sales campaigns and lead generation campaigns side by side on FB. I understand the value of building a list but my end goal is sales…so…

The Ad to Sales Page "Hacker" method is great!

Now, I know if you're just starting out the thought of actually *gasp* selling something probably scares the living daylights out of you…

But isn't that what you want to do? Isn't that the main reason you bought this book? Or did you just want a lot of people asking you questions all day that you answer for free?

Without going all "guru" on you…you need to upgrade your mindset.

Selling isn't evil or icky when you've got a quality product that actually helps people.

Selling is a service that helps people overcome their objections and make a decision that is in their benefit. Therefore, if you're selling something of quality that will benefit your target market you should get on with it. Anything else is insecurity and you need to get rid of it.

Be aware, the hacker method requires you to develop the two golden skills:

Traffic and Conversion.

Traffic is getting people to your page

Conversion is getting them to take action when they get there.

You don't have to be a world beater at either one but if you're just starting out you'll need a little of both.

I decided early on to use Facebook as my traffic source (more specifically paid traffic).

So, I learned how to run Facebook ads and make them profitable.

But you can use any method that suits you…doesn't have to be Facebook ads…

For conversion I focused on writing words that sell (copywriting) and I developed a rudimentary skill (growing all the time) in that discipline.

So the "Hacker" method as I do it depends on being able to create great ads and great sales letters. Here's a crash course:

Create great ads

Your ad is the "bait" that draws people to your sales page so it needs to be good. The right kind of ad will create massive curiosity for what you're offering and almost *force* people to click through. I recommend starting your ad with a question that calls out your ideal customer and catches their attention with a bold promise or claim.

Then tell your/a story to draw them to the CTA (call to action) to click the link and visit your page.

One thing that works really well is "teasing" the solution your product offers and telling the prospect to click to learn more about it. There's an old adage, "People love to buy but they hate to be sold." And I wholeheartedly agree with this!

Therefore, if your ad can create curiosity without necessarily presenting your product it's a win. For example, I run an ad for one of my products that talks about the solution the product provides without mentioning the product itself and asks people to click through to learn more.

This works really well because the call to action isn't a call to buy. It's a call to get more information about a subject they're already interested in. Then, once they're on the next page I provide value about the topic and give them an opportunity to buy if they want to take the next step!

The best direct response marketers know how to "sell" without selling. And this isn't a sneaky or underhanded thing to do. It has nothing to with "deceiving" or "tricking" people.

If you have integrity it means you believe your product will actually help your market, right? So, there's nothing wrong with presenting the information in a way that makes it fun and easy to make a buying decision. You're simply bypassing the skepticism that prevents most people from even getting to the buying decision phase.

Create great sales pages/letters

A sales page (or sales letter) is one of the most important parts of your business. And when you learn how to create ones that convert you'll have a huge advantage in whatever market you choose to serve.

The sales page is where you educate, inspire, and make your offer.

Typically, it will include these elements:

- **Headline**
- **Lead** (opening paragraph or sentence)
- **Story** (A story that sets up how you discovered the offer or a story about someone else that did and how it changed their life…)
- **Offer/Pitch** (Tell them what you have and what it's going to to for them)
- **Proof/Evidence/Testimonials**
- **Close** (Call to action with reason to buy now)

One of the best and easiest ways to create a great sales page is to format it as a letter, written directly to your customer. These are called Sales Letters and they're one of the most common formats for selling online or through the mail.

You've probably seen them before. I love sales letters because they're simple and you can tweak them until they convert at the level you're happy with then move on and let it sell for you. **(I've included a crash course on creating sales letters in Appendix 4 at the end of the book.)**

Practice Makes Perfect

Let's make it practical with an example using a $10 eBook applying the "Hacker" method.

So, you're not going to get rich selling a $10 eBook unless you've got LOADS of free traffic…

But I'm guessing you don't.

Therefore you'll need to pay for traffic.

Considering that traffic *ain't* cheap and $10 *ain't* much…you might not break-even selling something at that price.

But that's OK.

Because the Hacker method is about buying *customers* and the real money is made on the back end (selling other things to the people that have proven they're interested by actually buying something from you...).

Here's how it works:

- Facebook Ad promoting your book
- Sales page for $10 eBook
- Order bump $7 (another small offer people can just add on)
- Up-Sell of an Online Course $97 (up sell comes after the initial purchase)
- Email followup to buyers offering monthly membership $29

Let's say you launch your ads and your page and manage to sell 10 copies of your book for a $150 in advertising cost.

Oh no you lost money! You're a huge failure and everyone will laugh you to scorn...

Wait! We're not done...

Because 3 people (30% add the order bump) for an additional $21.

Then 1 person (10% purchase the upsell offer) buys the course for $97.

Let's do some math! (Never thought I'd say *that* happily...)

- After your 10 sales you've taken in $218. ($100 + $21 + $97)
- And you spent $150 on ads...
- **For a profit of $68!**

Pretty sweet right?

But here's what you've *really* done you titan of industry you...

You purchased 10 customers.

A GOLD mine.

Because now those 10 people have raised their hand and said, "We're EXTREMELY interested in what you've got to say!" They're practically begging for more.

Consider how *hard* it is for most people to actually pull out their credit card and purchase something.

Especially when they don't know you from Adam.

But they DID.

And that fact alone means something.

So, what next?

Well this is where the real magic of the "Hacker" method comes in.

Because now you've got a buyers list. It's time to use it.

A buyers list is where you put out your BEST.

This is where you give valuable training and content for FREE but with an invitation to ascend your customer ladder.

I recommend you figure out a continuity product ASAP and offer that to your buyers.

These folks have already *proven* their interest.

Remember the $29 membership I mentioned above?

This is where you want everyone to land!

And then stay forever…

Paying $29 per month of course.

Let's say that for every buyer you get 10% to sign-up for your membership.

So, working our same math from before…you've made a front-end profit of $68 and then an additional $29 for the membership for a total of $97. Not too shabby!

But remember that $29 membership is recurring so you're going to get that as long as they stay…

This is your "stick" rate. Let's say it's only 3 months on average. (you'll be able to figure out what it actually is when you're actually running your business).

3 months at $29 is $87

So add your $87 to the initial $218 in sales and you get $305 total revenue.

Minus the $150 you spent on ads…for a grand total of $155 profit free and clear!

But wait! There's more…(Gosh I love saying that)

Not only are you profitable, you can now turn around and reinvest that money into more ads…adding more customers into your business…

And, the people on your list are BUYERS.

But most of them just bought your $10 eBook.

So, you can sell them your order bump product, your course, and your membership as long as their on your list…

And many of them WILL buy.

So, there's no telling how much you'll make on the back-end.

But the beauty of this "Hacker" method is that when you do it right you've done the hard work up front: actually getting customers.

And then it's party time.

14

UNSOLICITED BUSINESS ADVICE FROM A GRIZZLED VETERAN

Alright, you snot-nosed little whippersnapper! *Pour yourself a drink and have a seat.*

I've got some advice for you that I had to learn the hard way.

The only thing that matters in business is achieving the end result.

Unfortunately, there are a ton of people confidently teaching how to do anything but actually make sales and make money. Ignore them.

Don't get caught up in chasing vanity metrics or complex guru nonsense being regurgitated on social media.

Clicks, likes, video views, and the all that don't *really* matter. They're a means to an end. So don't chase them…

Focus on making sales.

Turn those buyers into customers.

Then serve your people well. Defend and protect them. Give them excellent products and great customer support.

Rinse and repeat. You'll do fine.

That's why I recommend you start with the Hacker method for your first info-product and learn how to start selling right from the word *go*. Start with an offer priced between $5-$50 and start building a list of buyers right away.

A buyers list will ultimately be FAR more valuable and get you closer to your "1000 True Fans" than any vanity metric like a big list of leads. Buyers that become customers are the lifeblood of your business.

When I got started "everyone" was saying, "The money is in the list!" So, I of course assumed BIGGER is BETTER. Which is only half-true...

A bigger list of qualified buyers is better. But not necessarily a bigger list of leads.

Here's the thing...

90% (or more) of the people that find there way on your list aren't serious and **will probably never buy!**

So what if you didn't even bother with them?

...and believe me they *can be* a bother.

They'll ask questions, demand your time, and tax your patience.

You'll hold out hope that someday they might come around...and a few will but...

You need to count the cost. What's your time and focus worth to you?

Follow my advice and focus on creating a buyers list.

Let your friends with bigger (aka unprofitable leads lists) brag about how many subscribers they have while your small but mighty list of buyers and customers keeps kicking out sale after sale...

Here's how I look at advertising. When I spend money on traffic from Facebook or Google I'm investing in buyers. Buyers that can potentially turn into life-long customers.

I highly encourage you to do the same.

So let's boil it down to the bare minimum:

Just get an offer out there.

Whatever it takes, however bad you think it is, just do it.

1. Pick a market.
2. Create a product.
3. Turn it into an offer.
4. Put it on a website.
5. Send people there however you can.

G.K. Chesterton, one of the smartest guys that ever lived said,

> "If a thing is worth doing, it is worth doing badly."

The reality is you've got enough information in your hands (*I'm talking about this book knuckle-head*) to create a five or six-figure business if…

And that's a BIG *if*…

You push through your fear and do it!

15

HOW TO BUILD A LIST

One of the most important things to consider long term is your list.

A list refers to a list of names and emails (and potentially: addresses, phone, FB messenger, etc) that you can contact.

Unlike traffic from Facebook or Google. Your list is traffic you "own." These are people that have opted-in at some point and given you permission to contact them.

The great thing about having a list is that you "pay-once" to acquire them as a subscriber but then can communicate with them again and again as long as they stay subscribed.

My entire business strategy is based on getting people to subscribe then purchase then purchase again. Whenever I approach a new market I'm looking to accomplish 3 things (hopefully at the same time!)…

- Build a list
- Make sales
- Create customers (repeat buyers)

Here are a few ways to build a list:

1. The Slow Way - Content Marketing and Organic Traffic

The slow way consists of creating content that functions as "bait" for your target audience. Things like: blogs, podcasts, videos, social media posts, etc. Then somewhere within that content or at the end you invite people to join your list, i.e., give you their email.

There's nothing wrong with this method and it's perfect for people that are cash poor and time rich. Furthermore, your content functions as a "pre-qualifier" and ensures that the people signing up for your list are in fact interested in your topic.

Then you can sell your product via email down the line.

2. The Fast Way - Paid Traffic

The "Fast" way of building a list utilizes things Facebook ads, Google Ads, or any number paid traffic sources to acquire leads.

This the primary way I build lists because I'm impatient and I value my time more than anything else.

Here's an example of how to build a list fast:

- Create a lead magnet that only your perfect prospect would want.
- Create a squeeze page where people can opt-in to your list in exchange for your lead magnet.
- Run a targeted Facebook ad offering your lead magnet that goes to your squeeze page.
- Watch the leads roll in!

Now, with paid traffic you'll need to "know your stuff" before you go hog-ape-wild...

You'll need to be aware of what it's costing you to acquire a lead and what that's worth to you.

So, you'll need to know some basic marketing concepts and terms such as:

- CPL (Cost per lead)
- CPC (Cost per click)
- CTR (Click-through rate)
- Conversion % (How many people that hit your page opt-in or buy)

These numbers have to work for you when using paid traffic. Your initial goal with paid traffic is to break even. If you can build a list and the list pays for it you're doing great!

The thing to remember when you're using paid traffic is that you need a monetization strategy on the back-end. Unless you've got money to burn which I'm guessing you don't...

So, before you turn on the traffic floodgates, have a plan and process for making money from your list.

So...

- Build a list
- Sell them something
- When they buy, sell them something else!

My favorite list-building tactic when I'm using paid traffic is to create what's called a Self-Liquidating-Offer or S.L.O. for short.

The goal of a SLO is that you make enough money right away from your list to pay for the leads. And a properly executed SLO should work from day one when you launch your ads.

An S.L.O. is an offer you typically make to the people who opt-in for your lead magnet on the thank you page directly after opt-in.

One of my favorite SLO's uses "pay what you want" pricing.

What's that you ask?

I shall divulge but only because you asked so politely...

It simply means offering a product and letting the customer pay whatever they want!

Not every online cart allows you to do this but SamCart does. You can check it out at: www.boringoldbusiness.com/tools

I typically put a minimum of $1 but that's basically nuthin' *right*?

What's cool is that some people pay $1 but others pay $5, $20, and even $50 depending on what you offer.

The main thing is it needs to be a "no-brainer" offer even if it's low-ticket. Some might say *especially* because it's "low-ticket" because sometimes that's even harder to sell believe it or not...

But this is a quick way to pre-qualify people and build a buyers list which I recommend you do.

And psychologically it feels like you're doing them a favor. Because you've given them some autonomy and decision-making power which advanced persuasion ninjas will recognize as something important when it comes to negotiation and sales...

Let's Talk About Lead Magnets

When it comes to list building the most important part is your lead magnet.

A lead magnet can be a PDF, Webinar, eBook/Book, video, or anything else that someone is willing to exchange their email or other contact info for.

But, it all starts with the lead magnet.

Here are some governing principles when it comes to creating the perfect lead magnet.

- Is something only your perfect prospect would want
- Specific

- Easy to consume
- Provides a quick win
- Leads naturally to your next product or offer

One thing to remember is that your lead magnet should actually work like a real magnet which has a positive and a negative pole. Meaning, it should *attract* and *repel* at the same time.

A great lead magnet shouldn't be something *everybody* wants because *everybody* isn't your market. So you need to be strategic with what you offer people to join your list.

Here's a horror story to wake you up...

Right now it's popular to build lists using a giveaway or sweepstakes entry. You get entries for sharing the contest with others and everyone puts their email or contact info in to register.

People have been able to build massive lists FAST with this technique. But here's the problem.

That massive list is most likely a pile of hot-steaming garbage.

Those aren't buyers or even potential buyers that are interested in what you have to offer.

They're freebie seekers looking to get lucky.

And a list full of those people is almost guaranteed to be mediocre and unresponsive.

Here's the dark side you don't hear about. What's going to happen when you start emailing those people with your offer?

A bunch of them are going to hit the SPAM button and complain!

If you get enough complaints, there's a chance you'll get flagged and get your email service shut down.

So, consider what type of fish you want to catch before you bait the hook and throw it in the water!

That's why the first step to a good lead magnet is to make sure it only attracts the type of person you actually want on your list.

One of the most popular formats for a lead magnet is a pdf that provides value in some form like a checklist, report, etc.

They're easy to create, distribute, and consume. And, you can launch an entire business with just one good lead magnet.

But here's what I think you should do instead that will make the "provide value - give before you ask" crowd go crazy with rage…

Sell Your Lead Magnet

That's right. I said it.

Sell it. Don't give it away.

What Jake? But no one will buy it! I'll look like a greedy jerk!

Wrong.

One of the smartest marketing principles is to always ZIG when everyone else ZAGS.

Do the opposite of what EVERYONE else is doing.

And right now, everyone is offering a FREE lead magnet. *And we're all sick to death of it…*

It's an avalanche of FREE.

But watch this.

free free free free free free free free free free free free PAID free free free free free free free free free free free free VALUABLE free free free free free free free free free free free free free free free free free free free free free free free REAL EXPERT free free free free free free free free UNIQUE free free free free free free free free free free free EXCLUSIVE free free free free free free free free free free free free free

What sticks out?

As my dad always says, "In the land of the blind, the one-eyed man is king."

Be different and be bold enough to have the audacity to demand payment for your highly valuable information…and watch what happens?

Sure you'll get less opt-ins than freebie Freddy down the lane…but you'll have a list of buyers and customers. Which in the end is the real goal.

OK, is there ever a use for free lead magnets?

Absolutely!

Like everything in life the answer is it depends.

I've used free lead magnets with success.

And every market is different.

But my point remains. Zig when they zag and you'll do well because the hardest part of business is getting noticed. With that said, make sure and test different list building strategies (free, paid, SLO) and combine them to see what works best for your business.

Take this advice and go build a great list!

16

CREATING A PRODUCT ECOSYSTEM

Ok, what does this even mean?

Lean in my eager pupil and allow me to further enrich the soil of your verdant mind…

First a simple definition of the term "ecosystem":

> "A community of living organisms together with the nonliving components of their environment, interacting as a system." (https://simple.m.wikipedia.org/wiki/Ecosystem)

My dead simple definition: "A symbiotic, self-contained system of interconnected parts."

An ecosystem is a self-contained environment where all needs are met. A product ecosystem has an answer for everything your customer wants/needs.

Think about this. A business serves a purpose. It solves a problem for the customer. There are some businesses that serve diverse customers but most have a particular prospect. And if you think through all the solutions your prospect needs you can create a product for each and every one of them.

Here's why this matters to you and your business.

When you're able to create an ecosystem of products you'll be able to bring customers into it and they'll never have to leave! And if you do it right…they won't want to.

This is a sound business strategy because it's harder to acquire new customers than keep existing ones.

Think about this progression.

- You've invested time, energy, and money into your product.
- You've researched your market like a madman.
- You've put in blood, sweat, and tears figuring out how to market and sell it.

And at the end of all of that…if everything goes correctly…you get a customer.

What most people do at this point (including me…what a moron I've been…) is get happy feet and want to go start ALL OVER in another market…

Grass looking greener my friend?

Let me save you a lot of trouble with this friendly advice: Don't. Be. An. Idiot.

Figure out how to create a product ecosystem that leverages all the work you've already put in!

Here's a perfect example of a product ecosystem.

Our favorite fruit company: APPLE.

> "Need a computer? Here's a Mac. Will that be laptop or desktop? More power or less? And oh yeah, want fries with that…I mean RAM with that? How about a computer in your pocket that

makes calls and takes pictures? Here's your iphone...that'll be $1,300 please. Oh, want something that's not quite a computer but not a phone? iPad coming right up! Gosh, with all those nice devices you'll need music, TV, and movies to play on them. Step right through here…"

See it now?

It's like the Hotel California…you can check in anytime you want but you can't ever leave. And as a happy Apple customer I don't even want to…

So, how can you apply this information in your business?

Here's how to build a product ecosystem:

- Know your market better than it knows itself.
- Anticipate their problems and desires.
- Create products that solve them.
- Position products strategically so they lead into each other and work together.

That last part is where the magic happens.

Because eventually you can spend more time creating products for existing customers than you do acquiring new ones (which is harder to do…).

Question: *Can this be done with other business models? What about businesses that don't sell physical products?*

The Apple computer example of a product ecosystem obviously deals with mostly physical products. So can it be executed with info products?

Short answer: Yes.

Longer one: Still yes but here's why…

Consider my info product business that provides training for pastors and churches. There are numerous problems and obstacles my customers face and they overlap to some degree.

So, to serve these people I need to anticipate their needs and solve their problems (sometimes before they even realize they have them). Then I can create products for my ecosystem. This allows people to happily buy whatever solution they need at the moment and then "discover" everything else I have to offer down the road.

Now, don't freak out about building a product ecosystem before you've created and sold your first product!

I simply wanted to give you wise guidance as you make progress.

So bookmark this chapter and come back to it after you're making sales.

Heed and grow wise!

17

DEALING WITH TECH

This chapter is going to save you so much time and money it's not even fair…

If I'd had *this book* when I started I'd be writing this to you from a villa somewhere on the Mediterranean…but I digress…

Finish reading the chapter and then head over to:

www.BoringOldBusiness.com/tools

One of the biggest obstacles to aspiring INFOpreneurs looking to sell what's in their head is the technology involved.

I hear it a lot…"I'm not techy enough…and on and on."

I get it. But there's literally NO reason to let the fear of technology stop you from accomplishing your goals.

Especially because we're living in a time when every single tool we need is at our fingertips and easy to use!

When it comes to tech I built my business almost exclusively with one tool: **KAJABI**

Ka-what-bee?

Let's say it aloud together: *Cuh-Jah-BEE*

Kajabi!

You've got it! It's fun to say and even more fun to use.

Here's how they describe themselves:

"Kajabi is an all-in-one platform that makes it easy to create online courses, launch marketing campaigns, build landing pages, and design the perfect website."

What you really need to know is that you can literally build your ENTIRE online business using this ONE tool.

I am a passionate user and promoter of Kajabi because my success as an INFOpreneur wouldn't have been possible without them.

Beyond having the best tools available their customer support is legendary.

24/7 chat support and a robust community of users provide an incredible experience. With Kajabi, you're never left alone…

With this one tool you get:

- Website
- Blog
- Landing Pages
- Email Autoresponder
- Online Cart and Payment Processing
- Unlimited Wistia Video Hosting
- Course/Product Hosting
- Marketing Pipelines (Funnels)
- Quiz and Assessment Builder

Literally, *everything you need* in one place.

And at a fraction of the price if you bought it all individually.

Believe me I tried.

So, no more excuses about tech stopping you from selling what's in your head!

Grab a FREE 28 day trial at: www.boringoldbusiness.com/tools

With Kajabi you can literally start your journey as an INFOpreneur right now. Pretty awesome.

Additional Tech-Tools:

While I HIGHLY recommend starting with Kajabi there are several other tools I've used and recommend as well depending on your needs.

Online Shopping Cart:

SamCart

SamCart is an online shopping cart platform and sales page builder that has taken my business to another level!

And if you've already got a website or online presence of any kind I'd grab this and go to town. Your shopping cart is one of, if not the, most important parts of an online business. It's where people actually pull out their card and buy.

SamCart has great support, rock-solid and secure tech and advanced features that make it AMAZING to use like dunning (payment recovery), capturing abandoned cart emails for followup (literally adds money back into your account…), payment plans, order bumps, upsells and upsell funnels, product delivery, native integration with Kajabi and Convertkit, FB pixel tracking, and more…gosh I love it.

I've started building my sales pages right in SamCart with their new page builder and sending traffic right from Facebook (hacker method baby!) and it works so well!

Plus, SamCart will even deliver files/folders up to 1GB right to your customers which is a dream for eBook and course creators...

No messing with confusing passwords and logins for your customers...

There's a time and a place for having a membership portal that's password protected but not when you're selling a $37 eBook. It's just an unnecessary hassle IMHO.

Grab a free trial of SamCart at:

www.BoringOldBusiness.com/tools

Email/Autoresponder:

First tip...not MAILCHIMP..just...no...

For email I am a HUGE fan of ConvertKit. I use them for my email needs even though Kajabi has a full featured great email tool that's included with your subscription. I was a Convertkit user before I found Kajabi so I stayed with what I knew...but if you're just starting out I recommend using Kajabi so you can save some money.

What sets ConvertKit apart from the pack is the price (they're one of the most affordable) and the U.I. (user interface). It's very easy to use even though there are powerful features like automation and sequences.

For the most budget conscious INFOpreneurs you could actually start and operate a whole business via email with Convertkit.

You could run traffic to an opt-in and then have email sequences deliver your marketing and product content!

Just an idea.

To properly run the "hacker" method I recommend using a combo of Samcart and ConvertKit.

Grab a free trial of Convertkit at:

www.BoringOldBusiness.com/tools

Landing Pages:

If you're not using Kajabi then you'll need a basic landing page and funnel builder. For this I recommend Click Funnels. There are a lot of options but Clickfunnels is the industry leader for a reason. It's kind of a jack of all trades master of none product that has everything an online entrepreneur needs. I like to use CF to test new ideas and workflows. Because it does a little of everything it's perfect for this.

Grab a free trial of ClickFunnels at:

www.BoringOldBusiness.com/tools

Webinars:

I've run my auto webinar with Easywebinar since the beginning and it's been great. There's a definite learning curve with this software and it's not pretty (it's honestly butt ugly...haha) but it's the most powerful and cost-effective solution on the market IMHO.

At the risk of sounding like a broken record - just start with Kajabi even if you want to do an auto webinar distribution model because you can host video on Kajabi and create an auto webinar "like" experience for people.

But, if you're going all in on webinars you need Easywebinar.

You know the drill right?

Head on over to:

www.BoringOldBusiness.com/tools

Scheduling:

At some point you'll want to set up meetings and just allow people to schedule it themselves in your predetermined schedule. For that, you can use Calendly! It's cheap - simple - and very helpful!

Meetings/Coaching Calls:

For online meetings or coaching calls ZOOM is the cream of the crop. It's easy to use - works really well - and it's affordable to host meetings! There's even a free option to start.

Well, even though this chapter was short and to the point it can honestly save you hundreds of hours and thousands of dollars. Why mess with success when you can learn from my mistakes and just start with the best tools available?

You can literally get your whole business off the ground with these tools.

So what are you waiting for?

Go check out the TOOLS page at:

www.BoringOldBusiness.com/tools

And go for it!

18

ELIMINATING LIMITING BELIEFS

One of the most important factors in a brain based business is...you guessed it...YOUR BRAIN!

Well, more specifically, your mind.

Before you win "out there" you have to win "in here." This means beating the limiting beliefs that paralyze you and cause you to fail before you even begin.

- Fear of failure.
- No one will want my product.
- I'm not good enough.
- I don't have enough time.
- I don't have enough money.
- It's too hard.
- It takes too long.
- I don't have any ideas.
- I'm not smart enough.
- It's too risky.

All of these limiting beliefs will hold you back from achieving your goal of selling what's in your head! You've got to beat them down. Here's an encouragement for you.

Every great infopreneur struggles with limiting beliefs and fear.

Every. Single. One.

Don't believe for one second that the uber-confident guru you follow on Facebook has it all together. They don't. They've simply learned to move the limiting beliefs to the back of the line.

They choose to move forward even when they're afraid. It takes courage. Courage isn't the absence of fear. It's choosing to act in spite of fear.

If you want to make it in this business you'll need to beat your fear and insecurity into submission. And, I know you can do it!

Let's tackle a few of them together shall we?

Fear of failure.

This is the root of all limiting beliefs.

"What if I fail?"

Embarrassment. Shame. Humiliation. The end of the world!

Not so much...

Let's take this on.

I've heard fear described as, "false evidence appearing real."

And along those lines here's my definition of fear:

Fear is fantasy masquerading as reality.

Unless you know the future you have no idea what will happen until you try. If you do happen to know the future you have a killer product that you should be marketing right now!

Fear is an illusion of failure in the same way that delusion is an illusion of success.

Until you try something you simply don't know if it will work or not.

But here's what you *can* know for sure. If you follow fear you'll fail every time.

Fear is a self-fulfilling prophecy.

"I don't know if this will work so I won't try…"

See what I mean?

But don't just take my word for it!

Listen to the great hockey-haired hero of yore, Mr. Wayne Gretzky, who said, "100% of the shots you don't take don't go in."

Legendary hockey player and brilliant philosopher. Geez, some people get all the talent, right?

Here's the bottom line. Fear will paralyze you and cause you to fail before you even start. You've got to deal with it before it takes control. Make a determination right now to take action on at least one of your ideas and see it through to completion.

Yeah, it might fail. Or it might not.

But you'll never know until you try.

You also won't learn anything. And that's what fear *really* steals from you…the opportunity to learn. Successful infopreneurs ignore fear and embrace failure because even when your worst fears come true you can learn from what went wrong.

Here's the last word on the fear of failure.

I've never met a successful person that didn't have the ability to conquer fear and embrace failure.

You. Will. Fail.

Until you don't…

Don't let fear stop you before the journey even starts.

∼

The next limiting belief we'll deal with is this…

"What if no one wants my product?"

This one's pretty easy to knock down.

There are over 300 million people in the United States alone.

There are 7 billion humans on the planet.

At least one of them wants what you have.

Don't believe me?

Did you know there are people making a multiple six-figure income selling info products about knitting? I've personally sold hundreds of thousands worth of books, courses, and coaching packages to pastors and churches that want to grow. I know a lady who makes $600 a month selling a book about a particular breed of dog on Amazon…without advertising at all. SMH.

People *want* to buy stuff. They *want* to learn stuff. They *want* entertainment. And now you can present *your* thing to them while they surf the web in their pajamas and eat Cap'n Crunch!

The sheer volume of humanity paired with the instantaneous access the internet provides is on your side. If you have something that has any value at all…you can sell it.

"Ok, ok. But I'm not the best at what I do. I'm not an expert. Why would someone want *my* thing?"

Here comes a principle about life and business that's worth whatever you paid for this book.

It's called the "One-Step Ahead" principle and it goes like this…

You only need to be one-step ahead.

That's it. Maybe your brain didn't explode with the profundity of that but stay with me.

You don't need to be Tony Hawk to teach a kid who's never ridden a skateboard how to do an ollie.

You don't need to be Martha Stewart to teach someone to poach an egg and serve brunch.

You don't need to be Eric Clapton to teach someone to play a G-chord on the guitar.

You don't need to be Luke Skywalker to teach someone how to use a lightsaber...well that last one might not be true but...you get it...

One step ahead. That's it.

Here's the thing.

Most people actually prefer learning from someone closer to their level.

When I got into this business of selling info-products I kind of shied away from the dudes who were like, "I make 90 trillion dollars an hour selling ice to eskimos and drive a gold plated Lambo..." It was too intimidating when I was just starting out.

So I connected with a few mentors via the web that weren't as far ahead of me. I watched them and followed their moves. Some were just one step ahead. But I appreciate them because they cast some light on the way forward.

That's the beauty of this business model.

There's always someone at a different step of the journey in whatever niche or industry you're in. Maybe you're only at step two or three. Your customer is the person at step one.

Just stay one step ahead. Or don't! You could literally create one product that helps people take one step! And, that product can really help people and make you a lot of money in the process.

Take a second and think about one step you could help someone take…there's a business in there somewhere!

Plus, and this is a BIG plus, you've got this book…it's like Dumbo's magic feather!

If you aren't familiar with Dumbo's magic feather you need to go watch the old classic Disney version…like right now! "I'm not crying…*you're* crying!"

In a nutshell, Dumbo is an elephant with HUGE ears that give him the ability to fly.

But he doesn't believe in himself so his friend, a talking mouse (sounds unbelievable when you write it but it's definitely a true story…), gives him a "magic" feather and tells Dumbo it gives him the power of flight.

Needless to say, the feather gives Dumbo the confidence and belief to take the leap of faith and trust in his abilities. He didn't need the feather to fly but it gave him the power to overcome his fear.

And you're holding a magic feather right now!

Except this book actually does contain some real magic.

If you follow the steps in this book you know how to:

- Choose and validate a market
- Create products and "no-brainer" offers.
- Set up a selling process.

That information will take you far if you put it into action.

Now it's time to fly!

∾

"Ok, but even if people want what I have they won't actually buy it…I learned it for free."

This one's easy to knock down.

Even if you learned what you're selling for free people will still buy it from you because you're not just selling the information itself.

You're selling a shortcut.

Or a better tool.

Or making their life easier.

Or...whatever...

Almost every successful business has an angle like this.

You've invested the necessary time and energy to acquire the steps to achieve something. Maybe they can learn it for free by spending 10 hours watching YouTube. Well, you've done that for them and now they can learn the same thing in only 4 hours from you. You're providing the value of time-saving.

People will absolutely pay for convenience. Don't forget it.

If someone makes $25 an hour than you've saved them $150. If you sell that information for $75 they're getting a great deal and so are you! They've saved time and money and learned something useful. You put in the time and energy once and now you can sell it again and again.

Let's break it down a little further.

Imagine you're selling an info-product that teaches people how to organize their closet in a specific way. Not only does this method (that you learned from your crazy grandma or something...haha) save people time but it also allows them to reclaim wasted space in their closet.

Can you mine that concept for the potential value it provides?

First, as we just discussed...it saves people time.

Time is the most valuable commodity because it's truly finite. Anything that saves people time has tremendous value.

Second, it helps them reclaim space in their closet/house.

That's real estate right there. You've helped them get back square footage that they were missing out on. If they paid $125 a sq. ft for that space and you can give 1 or 2 of it back to them it's worth $125-$250 dollars!

Third, it makes them *feel* better because now their stuff isn't piled on the bed, laying on the floor, or blocking a hallway.

They have space to live, work, play, eat, read, or whatever. You've helped them declutter and simplify their life. What's that worth? Depending on your ability to describe and sell it…a lot!

Starting to see the possibilities here?

These concepts are incredibly important to grasp as you structure an offer for your info product. Don't sell features. Sell benefits. Talk about how much time and money people will save with your product. Tell them how their life will be better. Tell them what results they'll get!

As a wise old marketer once said, *"We don't sell the hammer or nail…we sell the hole!"*

If you do that you won't have a problem selling what's in your head.

～

"But I don't have the time!"

The last limiting belief we'll smash to pieces is about your capacity.

Specifically as it relates to time.

Almost everyone I talk to about the potential of creating an info-product uses a lack of time as an excuse.

"I'm just so busy…"

"I work a *real* job."

"With my husband and kids…it's so busy…"

"I'm just so tired when I get home from work…"

"I don't have the head space for creating…"

C'mon people!

Do you know what the problem with excuses is?

They work.

Unfortunately what happens is they excuse you from success.

Is that what you really want?

You need to admit something to yourself: **Nobody has more time than you.**

We've all got 24/7/365. Some people just use their time better than others.

So stop complaining and take control of your life.

Sure, I understand that everyone has different circumstances but don't make excuses. Make changes and make something of yourself. Because if you really want to do something you can *make* the time to get it done…and I'll show you how.

Many people also try to explain to me why I'm different…

"Oh, Jake you're able to do the things you do because you're smart, or gifted, or…yada yada yada…"

I usually stop listening when I hear people try and figure out the secret of my success because they're almost always wrong and I already know what it is…

And, I'll tell you what it *really* is in a minute but keep reading because I'm dropping wisdom bombs on you that are worth whatever the H-E-Double-Hockey-Stick you paid for this book right now…

Let me give you the time-tool you can use to break the piss-poor thinking and economic chains off your life.

The only thing you need to do is **buy back one hour a day for yourself.**

This means doing whatever it takes to free up one single hour per day that you *ruthlessly* protect and relentlessly invest in thinking, writing, creating, or building your info-product.

This hour belongs to you and you alone. It's not for entertainment, distraction, or other people.

Essentially, this one hour daily investment is your ransom payment to the universe to get you off the "time for money" hamster wheel…

You've heard it said, "Time is money?"

Right. Well, that's not exactly true.

Time isn't money. Time is life. More specifically *your* life. And it's slipping through your fingers right now…

The problem is that most people are in fact trading their life for money ($10-$20/hour) which is astonishing to me….because is that *all* their life is worth to them? *To you?*

If so, and you're happy trading your life for a few bucks an hour go find a smart looking person and sell this book to them…maybe they'll use it!

Or, if you're like me and *refuse* to trade your life for a few measly bucks an hour then pay attention.

So, how do you buy back an hour?

Easy.

Remember Benjamin Franklin?

Well he was the wise chap that said, "Early to bed and early to rise, makes a man healthy, wealthy, and wise."

Early to bed. Early to rise.

That's your ticket to freedom…how *you* can buy back an hour a day to invest in your future.

Go to bed one hour earlier (sacrificing social media, TV, and other brain-rotting pastimes) and wake up one hour earlier. That's it.

Then use that extra hour whenever you're at your best (during the day) to create and build assets (like an info-product for instance) that you can use to make money that you don't have to trade your life for.

Check this out. I think this will blow your mind…

If you use your "one-hour" to write and can write 500 words an hour (half of what professional writers can do) you'll have written 50,000 words in only 100 days. That's a good sized non-fiction book!

So, let's say you do that 3 times a year…

You've now written 3 books. With 65 days to spare…

What if you write shorter books like the kind I recommend earlier that you can sell for $20-$50? In just an hour a day you could write six 30,000 word books or twelve 15,000 word books.

And let's say you're able to sell two or three of those books per day to someone online…

You've got a business on your hands and you only invested an hour a day.

Hate writing?

No problem.

Use that hour to map out your online course, create an outline, and then start making videos. Plan your lesson on Monday. Film it on Tuesday. Edit it on Wednesday. Upload it on Thursday. And so on…

If you put out a lesson per week you'll have a 10-week Masterclass in about…*is the suspense killing you*? You guessed it! 10 Weeks!

Do that 3 or 4 times per year?

Again, you've got a business on your hands and you only invested an hour a day.

One. Hour. Per. Day.

What are you waiting for?

~

OK, the secret to my success? I know you're just *dying* to know…

It's not brilliance or innate giftedness.

It's much simpler than that…

I just keep working on stuff until I'm done with it.

And early to bed, early to rise…buying back an hour (and eventually more)…has allowed me to get off the "time-for-money" hamster wheel.

And you can do the exact same thing.

But you've got to stop making excuses and start with buying back one hour a day that you invest in creating.

19

FROM HOBBY HUSTLER TO BUSINESS BARON

Ok, this chapter might not be for you...

If you're happy just making a little extra cheddar every month and you LOVE your day job just stop reading.

This chapter is for the pedal to the metal crowd that wants to go full time as an INFOpreneur. World domination type stuff...you get it.

So, last warning...turn back unless you're serious about transforming from a side-hustling amateur to a titan of info industry!

In actuality...even if you just want to create a profitable side-hustle this is for you!

Remember the story I told you earlier about selling my books on Amazon?

At first I was just excited that people wanted to buy my book and that Amazon could help me sell it through their paid ads platform. I'd never been able to sell very many books through my organic marketing efforts and now I had the ability to buy ads, drive traffic to my book, and make some sales!

I learned a LOT from this. I learned how valuable a good cover is, how important your book description is, and I started to learn the science of selling psychology.

It was fun and a great learning experience!

But then I got massively frustrated...

There I was, paying Amazon good money to advertise my book, then paying them a commission on every sale of my book, and at the end I had a sale but no customer. No email address to follow up with. No way to talk to the people that bought my book.

I realized I had a hobby, not a business. I had a side-hustle.

I traded a little time for a little money. It was the digital equivalent of a pizza delivery job.

I'm not knocking that at all but it wasn't really what I was after.

Selling my book at $3.99 wasn't going to amount to much if I couldn't scale my sales or stay connected with my customers. It's not a knock on Amazon. They're a great company and they're smart because they know the money is in the customer.

It wasn't Amazon's problem. It was mine. It was time to level-up and learn what it would take to really sell what was in my head.

I decided then and there that I wasn't going to spin my wheels trying to move $3 eBooks for the rest of my life. That's when it hit me.

I had learned to use *paid* traffic to sell information (my eBook). My problem wasn't the model. It was the price and the process. I decided to create a new info product at a higher price point and become my own Amazon (distributor/marketplace). I would control the advertising, the sale, distribution, and build a relationship with my own customers.

I started tuning in to some of the "legends" of marketing. People that are phenomenal at creating, communicating, and selling information!

And, I noticed they shared a few things in common.

- A predisposition to action.
- A focus on list building.
- A strategic approach.

Let's look at these 3 factors as we discuss building a knowledge based business.

Action-Oriented

Isn't there a semi-successful shoe company with a slogan like, "Go For It…or Just Move On…or…?"

Just Do It.

What separates the real players from the posers in the knowledge industry is a radical predisposition to action. The ones that make money and really help people in the process don't wait around to get stuff done. They favor production over perfection. If they have a killer idea they don't wait for permission. They kick doors down to get it done.

They don't stop when it gets hard or when they encounter obstacles. They relish it. They eat the challenge for breakfast and the leftovers for lunch. They are action-oriented doers who don't allow fear to paralyze them.

You're going to need at least a little of that bent.

Now, if you're like me that doesn't come naturally. I've had to embrace this mentality. I am a perfectionist by nature. Many times when I'm writing I'll be paralyzed with indecision over a particular word or phrase.

"Could I say it better?"

"Period or comma here?"

"Is this a run on sentence?"

You get it.

Unfortunately, perfection is the mortal enemy of progress.

If your goal is to create the Mona Lisa of $39 eBooks then by all means, parse every word like your life depends on it.

If, on the other hand, your goal is to help people solve problems, get your ideas into the world, and make some money in the process then you need to get stuff done.

Building Your List

The next thing I learned was that to have a business I needed to have an ongoing relationship with my customers. The mantra I heard again and again was, "The money is in the list." This took me awhile to understand but now it's become clear.

Your social media, amazon sales, itunes downloads, etc. are all happening on someone else's digital real estate. You might be making good sales but until you connect with and own your own customer base you'll always be a renter.

And renters get evicted…

When Facebook changed their algorithm several years ago and stopped giving Pages the organic reach they were used to it left a lot of them in the lurch. Businesses and brands that had gone all out to get page likes found themselves cut off at the knees, their ability to connect with and communicate to their own audiences severed.

The brands that had gone about doing the hard (and sometimes boring) work of getting emails and staying in contact with their list were fine. The Facebook change was a blip. Their business wasn't built on rented (digital) real estate. They owned their own land, as it were.

The money is in the list.

What money?

I've heard it said that each email subscriber you have on your list is worth around $1 per month. So if you have 100 subscribers that should be worth around $100 a month to you. I have found this ratio to be pretty accurate but not in the way I originally thought. For me, the majority of my sales come from a small subset of my list (buyers) but it tends to average out to around $1 per month per subscriber.

What I've since learned is that my list tends to adhere to the ubiquitous 80/20 principle. 80% of the results come from 20% of the list. And it's not hard to figure out what seperates the 20% from the rest. They're the buyers/customers. So now I'm predominantly focused on growing THAT segment of my list.

Because I know people that have MASSIVE email lists and don't make any money.

What gives?

Two words…**list quality**.

There are two factors that make all the difference when it comes to lists.

The first one is **targeting**.

If your list is filled with people that have no interest in what you do (or no intent to buy) than the ratio won't hold up. Some people do all kinds of things to get friends, family, and random strangers on their list. But other than making you feel good about your numbers this has no value.

You want targeted, pre-qualified people who are super into whatever it is you do on your list.

It might build your confidence when your aunt responds to your email and says, "Great job honey…" but if she's not buying she doesn't need to be on the list.

So, the name of the game isn't just building a massive list. It's building a massive list of customers and potential customers.

The second thing you must do with your list is actually sell something to it. **You need a product or service**!

Believe it or not, there are people out there with email lists that they write to regularly and yet don't sell anything. *Do they just really enjoy writing emails?*

At some point you're going to have to just get over your fear, create or find a product, and actually ask someone to buy it! That's what the pros do. And you know what? Your list will thank you for it because you're making products and services that make their lives easier/better!

I'm not angry at Apple for asking me to buy the laptop I'm writing this book on right now. I'm not mad at my local coffee shop for letting me know there's a delicious scone and a hot cup of joe waiting for me inside. *I'm grateful...*

All of us have money that we WANT to exchange for value. Good business isn't about tricking or manipulating people. Good business is about connecting supply and demand. Everyone walks away happy! Everybody wins. That's good business.

A Strategic Approach

This is probably the most important of the three factors I'll discuss in this chapter. Pros don't just sell products. They work a process. They're strategic.

They think about the long term not just the short term.

What really separates businesses from hobbies is the planning that goes into creating a process. Here's the thing, for every "rags to riches" story you hear about some guy without a plan starting a business in his garage that becomes a success there's a million stories you don't hear where he fails catastrophically.

Think about it.

Everyone loves a winner! Nobody cares about the business that one dude *tried* to start.

So, before you think about what product you could make just to make money short-term, take some time and consider the long game.

Ask yourself some clarifying questions:

- What am I passionate about?
- What can I do to really help people?
- What is unique about me or my brand?
- Is this something I'd be happy to do for at least a few years?

Once you've answered these questions start thinking about building a long-term strategy.

- How will I generate traffic and build my list?
- What products or services will I create?
- How will I sell them?
- How will I serve my customers who've bought something from me?
- How will I deliver/manage my products and services?
- What is the end game here: my goal for this business?

Pros think through these questions right from the start. It might seem daunting but it will really help you in the long run. If you find a niche that you're passionate about and create products that really help people you will win in this business!

Then, there's the business side of this process. For that you only need 3 components (which I've mentioned before: traffic, conversion, and fulfillment)

- A way to consistently generate traffic/leads.
- A series of products (you can start with just one product but eventually you'll need more so that your customers can continue doing business with you).

- A way to serve and manage your business.

That's it.

The good news is this book is chalk-full of ideas for info-based businesses that you can take and use right away.

My encouragement to you is to emulate these pro tactics if you want to build a successful business that can go the distance!

20
WORDS OF WISDOM

So this is it, huh?

I've given you my best and now it's time for you to go make your way in the cold-hard world…

Well, it's been fun.

Allow me to leave you with a few words of wisdom before you ship out…

#1 - Persistence will take you farther than talent.

I'm not the best marketer, advertiser, copywriter, designer, writer, strategist, or businessman in my field.

I'm probably not even in the top 100.

But what does that matter?

I'm able to prosper because I'm in the game.

How many more talented/smarter/gifted people have never put their oar in the water?

As Thomas Edison famously said, "Genius is 1% inspiration and 99% perspiration."

Hard work with your head down will take you far.

Just remember, you can't lose if you don't quit.

Maybe your first info-product will be a huge success or maybe it won't.

Try, try again.

Just be persistent.

Learn. Try. Fail. Learn. Try. Succeed.

#2 - You're only competing with yourself.

Don't waste a moment looking left or right.

I've learned a few things along the way…

Most of the people that appear to be doing better than you are lying or there's more to the story that you're not aware of.

Comparison will snuff out your spark.

So don't do it.

And don't ever make someone else's success/failure the measure of your own.

If your "competition" is winning…*so what?*

Set your own goals and achieve them.

Your success will only come because you're working on your thing… not worried about someone else.

So spend your time, energy, and focus competing with yourself.

#3 - **Don't feed the trolls.**

Let's talk about about mean people, trolls, and critics?

Newsflash: You're going to encounter trolls.

And the more successful you are the more trolls you'll attract…like moths to a flame.

Because these people actually feed like parasites on the energy and output that successful people produce.

For whatever reason they've decided not to "produce" or "create" anything of their own and made it their mission to police, mock, and *troll* those that have.

They're the small-minded, jealous, and critical people who get their jollies "trolling" far more successful people.

They're the ones who feel obligated to fill the comment sections of Facebook and Twitter with criticism, sarcasm, and unsolicited advice (that's almost always wrong).

Most of the time these types of people are morbidly insecure about themselves and their lack of success.

You'll often spot them whining and complaining that you're charging for your products or services. They want everything for free but won't use it anyways…

They think pulling others down is how they pull themselves up.

If you're anything like what I've just described…take a long hard look at yourself and make a decision right now to run as fast as you can the other way.

Because if there's any part of you, ANY PART AT ALL, that's "troll-like" it will destroy your chance at success.

I had a mentor when I was in my late-teens who's nickname (I kid you not) was "Shanker."

John "Shanker" Gomez was a chicano from the wrong side of the tracks in Los Angeles. And he'd lived, let's just call it…a *colorful* life on the streets.

The guy was tough as hell, mean as a snake, and one of the best dudes you'd ever meet.

Later in life he became a mentor to young people like me.

And many times I'd come to him to complain about what other people were doing or saying and he'd snap like a whip, "What's that to YOU?!"

That would shut me up. Because I knew what he meant.

People are going to do what they're going to do.

Haters gonna hate.

Trolls gonna troll.

What's that to you?

Here's my mantra, "You can't control what other people do but you can control how you respond."

Don't be a troll and don't feed them.

Don't give them your time and attention.

Don't take criticism from people you wouldn't ask for advice *(saw that on a Morgan Freeman meme on Facebook one time)*.

Well, I've got more wisdom but I'm not giving it to you until you use what I've already given you…so go make it happen!

APPENDIX 1: THE "SELL WHAT'S IN YOUR HEAD" CHEATSHEET

Here's a cheatsheet with the 30,000 ft overview of how to *sell what's in your head*!

1. Choose your market (niche).

- Do your market research.
- Does this market have passion, money, and momentum?
- Are other people making money in this market?
- How are they selling?
- What are they selling? What are people buying?
- Amazon method (Look at the best-selling book list on Amazon in this market. Read the comments.)
- Google method (Use the keyword planner and the trending tool. Is there "mass" in this market?)
- Magazine method (Is there a long-running publication?)

2. Create your product.

- ebook
- Course

3. Build your "No-Brainer" offer.

- Add bonuses.
- Order bump - additional product offered at point of sale.
- Upsell - an offer that comes immediately after the initial purchase.
- Is there a continuity opportunity? (Membership, group, etc)

4. Create your sales page

- Be smart and use SamCart:
- www.boringoldbusiness.com/tools
- Headline
- Hook (opening paragraph or sentence…)
- Story
- Offer (Here's what I've got and what it can do for you!)
- Close (Make the dang sale.)

5. Build a list

- Use an inexpensive "paid" lead magnet to build a "buyers" list *or*…
- A free lead-magnet if you must.
- Drive traffic to the squeeze page that collects emails.

6. Create a product ecosystem and grow your business.

All the steps are there. Now it's just a matter of doing the work.

You'll need to learn and develop some skills along the way but I know you can do it. Just remember that you only lose when you give up.

As long as you keep trying you'll get where you want to go!

APPENDIX 2: HOW TO DO MARKET RESEARCH

Here's a crash course on doing a "heat check" of potential markets.

This will also allow you to "see" if your product idea is something that people in your target market might be interested in. Remember, we're looking to create products for markets that have already demonstrated a tendency to buy.

This becomes more useful for when you niche down…

The Big 3 hot markets have been and probably always will be Health, Wealth, and Romance because those are the basic human needs/desires.

And sub-niches in those markets should also do well.

Here are three proven market research tactics:

The Amazon Method

Here's how to use one of the world's most popular shopping sites to find out what your market is looking for.

Remember, you're looking for a market where people are already buying.

You can use the following trick to identify what types of products and information they're buying and then "reverse-engineer" it to create a profitable offer of your own.

- Examine the best-sellers list of books in your target market.
- What are people buying in that market?
- What is the title and topic of the #1 best-seller?
- Are there buzzwords in the comments?
- What problem is the best-seller offering to solve?
- What passion is it serving?
- What age group does it appeal too?
- Are there certain words and phrases you see in the titles and descriptions?

There is a veritable gold-mine of potential information here that you can use to create your product and position it as something people will want to buy! Study the comments like a detective looking for clues about your market.

The Google Method

Here's how to use the world's most popular search engine to find hot markets and products...

Use the Google keyword planner tool to find the search volume for keywords related to your product or market. This is a free tool that Google provides. You may need to create an Adwords account but it doesn't cost anything.

In this case, higher is better because that means more people are interested in your particular product. Make sure and look at the keywords and search strings Google suggests so you can get a good idea of what people are searching for.

This is a great way to see if people are "literally" looking for your product.

If you see that 100,000 people a month are searching for "how to train my dog" you know there's potential. Then it becomes an issue of creating the right product to serve that market.

Bonus points for drilling down and actually visiting the sites, forums, and sales pages where your market is going online.

The Facebook Method

Gosh, wouldn't it be great if there was a place where your market hung out all the time and talked about their pain, problems, interests, dreams, and desires in a totally unfiltered way?

Well you're in luck…it's called Facebook! And it's a marketers dream scenario…if you know how to use it.

Here are a couple of ways to get started:

- Join groups and just observe (as many as you can!)
- What are they saying? What are they bothered by? What words and phrases do they use?
- Find prospects from those groups and study them. Don't be a weird stalker but look at their interests. What books do they read? What movies do they watch? Who do they idolize or villainize? All of this information is like GOLD for you as you create your products and sales messages!
- Find pages that serve your market and analyze their content. What are people liking, clicking, and commenting on in your market?
- Look at as many pages, groups, and other places you can find within your target market and make a document of your observations. This will be something you can refer back to whenever you need info on your market. You'll also discover stories and examples you can use.
- Pro-Tip: You can actually "quote" what people say on

Facebook in your emails, sales copy, and products by saying something like, "I once saw this guy saying how much he hated going to the gym but still wanted to be ripped…and it made me think about how our supplement RX4500 would help him…" You're not mentioning the person by name but you can literally "use" your market's own words to sell back to them. See how powerful research can be?

The Magazine Method

Are there any popular, long-running magazines in your potential market?

If so, that means there are people willing to pay and some stability of desire in the market.

Obviously, health, wealth, and love are long-running and high potential markets. That's why there's many magazines and publications serving them.

But go online and search: "(your topic here) magazine" and see what comes up!

If there are established publications (magazines, newsletters, etc) that serve this niche it's because there is money in it. There are buyers to be found or people that are buying from the advertisers that use these publications.

Bottom Line

When you do market research your main goal is to identify the "hot buttons" in your market? It's what I call the emotional volcano… and your job is to make it erupt!

What are the triggers that, either positively or negatively, agitate the emotional volcano?

If you know what the triggers are you can use them to get and keep your market's attention and ensure that they'll be interested in your offers.

The big (or maybe obvious?) secret is that people don't buy because of logic. They buy because of emotion. The sooner you realize that and learn...

- What drives them crazy?
- What makes them angry?
- What makes them miserable?
- What makes them laugh?
- What makes them cry?
- Who do they hate? (Actors, politicians, ex boyfriends?)
- Who do they love? (See above!)
- What are their favorite books/movies?
- And on it goes...

...the sooner you'll know exactly what products to create and exactly how to sell them!

Great market research is the key to great products, great copywriting, and great results.

APPENDIX 3: "HACKER" COURSE SELLING METHOD CHEATSHEET

Here's the "Hacker" method I recommend for quickly bringing online courses to market…

This strategy alone can get you up to the $500-$5000 level of monthly revenue.

- Create your course (videos, pdf slides, and audio) and put it in a folder.
- Get a Samcart account (get their one-page funnel deal with the included training - it's GOLD). The offer on the webinar is for $997 but if you reach out to them they do have a $99 per month payment plan for this. You can also just wait for the email follow up where they eventually offer it for $99 per month.
- Create your "One-Page" Funnel.
- Price your course between $99-$299. Offer a limited time deal on your page (e.g., *The normal price is $199 but today you can get it for $99*)
- Offer one or more "bonuses" for people that purchase your offer e.g. a 30 minute coaching call, a private FB student

group, additional related content, worksheets, checklists, etc.
- Run a simple Facebook ad campaign sending traffic to your page. (Target interests related to your product and optimize for conversions.)
- Use Samcart to deliver your course automatically.
- Tweak your page until it makes more money than you spend on traffic.

Pro-Tip:

Price is only one factor that impacts sales. Lowering the price is almost never the best move. Try to INCREASE the value being offered before lowering the price. Use the 10x rule. Ask yourself, *"Is what I'm offering worth at least 10x the price?"* If not, add value until it is.

APPENDIX 4: SALES PAGE CRASH COURSE

One of the most important skills you'll need to develop is the ability to "sell" or "persuade" via print. For your digital info products to be considered "passive" income producers you'll need a sales page or what some call a sales letter to sell it for you.

The idea is that you send traffic to the page and 1%-10% of the people that visit actually purchase what's being offered!

The beautiful thing about this is once you've got a page that converts all you have to do is send traffic to it and watch the money roll in…

These are what I call "economic engines" that produce income for you without you actively "working" on it.

While that may sound like a pipe-dream it's totally possible. Because the principles behind what makes people buy are well-known.

So here's a 100 mph crash course…enough to make you dangerous!

Your sales page needs to accomplish a few things:

1. Give them a reason to buy.

- Show them how the product can solve a problem
- Show them how the product will help them fulfill a dream or desire
- Show them why the product is better than other options

2. Give them a reason to buy now.

- *This can be done with…*
- A limited time offer
- A deadline
- A sale
- Bonuses that expire
- An internal deadline - something they're missing out on right now by delaying
- *Urgency and scarcity are powerful but they have to be real otherwise they work against you.*

3. Show them evidence and proof.

- *You can give evidence and proof in a variety of ways including…*
- Testimonials
- Stories
- Quotes
- Research
- References

4. Create curiosity.

- Use bullets or "fascinations" to tease what's inside your product and create massive curiosity! And the late, great

copywriter Gary Halbert said, "Curiosity is the most powerful weapon of advertising…even more powerful than self-interest."
- Do your best to inject some curiosity into every part of your sales letter.

Page Format:

- Headline
- Lead (opening sentence or paragraph)
- Story
- Offer
- Close

This is a proven sales page structure. It's worked over and over again to sell ALL kinds of products, services, and training.

Here's a fictional example of a sales letter selling a rubber raft that I wrote in under 30 minutes…

Expert Wilderness River Guide Says, "This Is The Last River Raft I'll Ever Buy!"

Dear friend,

If you're sick and tired of constantly patching leaks in your rubber raft then you'll be excited to know about the Scout Raft 500 that utilizes a brand-new self-sealing rubber technology first developed by NASA scientists…

But first a story…

A few years back my wife talked me into going rafting with her and some friends. Not being an outdoorsmen myself I hesitantly agreed. Unfortunately our old raft that had been gathering dust in the garage had an undetected leak (common in regular rafts) and when we hit the first rapids it completely blew out!

Spilling us, our supplies, and our lunch into the raging river…

I was terrified for my life and even worse…felt helpless as I watched my wife struggle to keep her head above water…

Lucky for us the river split and we washed into a shallow channel where we scrambled up a black-berry bush covered bank!

A kind stranger took pity on us and drove us back to town with only our lives to show for our effort. I'll never forget how quickly and unexpectedly an afternoon that was supposed to be fun turned into a life and death situation…

But it wouldn't have happened if we'd been using the Scout 500 with self-sealing technology…

If you love to ride the rapids but your safety is important to you then the Scout 500 is the way to go.

That's why customer Ed Reed said, "I'd never put my family in another raft!"…after using the Scout 500.

And leading river guide Don Stevens has chosen the Scout 500 as the official kit for his award winning company: Adventure America.

So what are YOU waiting for?

Because right now you can get your hands on your very own Scout 500 River Raft for 50% off the regular price!

When you purchase a Scout 500 you'll receive…

- Leading proprietary self-sealing rubber technology first developed by NASA scientists for the international space station. This technology not only means your raft will never leak or tear…it keeps you and your family safe!
- The "deep well" design only found on the Scout 500 that creates a comfortable and stable "ride" as you travel on the river. Not found anywhere else…
- Six movable comfort foam seats so no-one has to argue over the best seat!

- Four high quality oars designed with our patented "featherweight" technology that makes them light as a feather but strong as iron. And they're covered under the lifetime warranty for workmanship and materials...The same you can read about right here...
- A lifetime warranty on materials. We're so confident in the quality and durability of the Scout 500 that we'll replace it FREE of charge if there's ever an issue with the build or materials.

With your purchase today you'll also receive some exciting bonuses:

Bonus #1 - "Reading White Water" - PDF

This practical guide is chalk-full of practical tips and wisdom from leading river guides on how to "read" the river. Something you read here might just keep you alive on your next river adventure. Value $39 - Your price: FREE

Bonus #2 - Electric Pump

With this electric pump you'll be able to inflate and deflate your new Scout 500 raft in mere minutes, saving you time so you can have more fun on the river! Value $99 - Your price: FREE

Bonus #3 - "Rivers of America" PDF

A full color guide listing all the most amazing river runs you can go enjoy with your new Scout 500. Value $29 - Your price: FREE

And today only you can get the Scout 500 for 50% off the regular price...

Normally the Scout 500 is $1999 which is still a great deal for the best raft on the market...

But for a limited time we're making the Scout 500 available for only $999.

And, including FREE rush shipping (lower 48 only) so you can get out on the river as soon as next week...

As you consider your options…

Remember, this is the **safest** and **most reliable** raft on the market.

Sure, you could save a few bucks picking up a cheap-rubber raft at your local big-box store but then **you'd be trusting your life to cheap rubber made by companies that care more about profit then your safety…**

And, not only is the Scout 500 safe.

It's comfortable!

The custom design insures your whole family (up to 6 people) can be comfortably seated as you enjoy the sights and sounds of the river…

So grab your Scout 500 today for only 50% off before they're gone!

BUY NOW BUTTON

———

As you can see in the short example above I included the elements necessary to make a sale. There was urgency and scarcity (50% off for a limited time). There was proof and credibility (expert river guide, NASA scientists, customer testimonial). There was excitement and curiosity.

Pro-Tips:

Price is only one factor that impacts sales. Lowering the price is almost never the best move. Try to INCREASE the value being offered before lowering the price. Use the 10x rule. Ask yourself, *"Is what I'm offering worth at least 10x the price?"* If not, add value until it is.

The best way to add value is by offering bonuses. Sometimes people buy the "core" product of the offer just to get access to one of the bonuses!

Bullet From The Blue

One "hack" to juice up your sales pages is to use bullets to "tease" and "fascinate" your product.

Here's what most people do with bullets:

Let's use a drill battery as an example…

Mack Co Drill Battery

- Long lasting 6 hour battery life.
- Lithium ion technology.
- Lifetime guarantee.

Now here's the "juiced" version:

- Long lasting 6 hour battery life…so your power tools will keep on working long after you've gone home for the day… Long lasting consistent power that just won't quit!
- Built with propietary lithium ion technology (developed by NASA scientists) that won't rust, corrode, or degrade…*EVER*. Say goodbye to the battery "build-up" that other manufacturers won't tell you about…
- Our "Built For Life" guarantee. We stand behind our products 100%. If there's ever a problem with your Mack Co battery just let us know and we'll fix it right away. So you can get back on the job…FAST.

See how those bad boys pack more of a punch?

Here's a little insight:

In the first bullet I added a benefit "Long lasting consistent power that just won't quit" to the feature "long lasting 6 hour battery life." The benefit tells the customer what the feature is going to do for them. You don't want to leave this up to their imagination. Spell it out.

In the second bullet I added a little authority and credibility with the "NASA scientists" and "proprietary" word. Obviously those would need to be true to work. So, look for facts about your products that bump up their credibility.

The second tactic I used was to mention a potential problem tool owners might not even realize they had…"battery build-up." What is it? What's it going to do? Who knows? But this battery doesn't do it!

In the third bullet I named the guarantee "Built For Life" to make it stick and give it personality. Great for branding. And, I added another benefit to the feature of the guarantee…"we'll fix it right away. So you can get back on the job…FAST."

Those bullets went from a 2 or 3 on the Richter scale to a 6 or 7 with just a few tweaks!

Go and do likewise!

APPENDIX 5: SELLING WITH WEBINARS

This is admittedly more *ninja* but I want to bring the HEAT in this book…so here we go!

Here's a powerful strategy I've used to get leads and customers using webinars.

Webinars can either be live or automated. And they both have pros and cons.

An automated webinar is just a pre-recorded training that almost always transitions into a pitch at the end just like a real webinar.

Automated is great because it's a passive, leveraged strategy.

Live webinars are great because you get to interact with your prospects and get real time feedback on your offer.

So which one should you use?

Both! - But I recommend you start with a live webinar.

Webinars are an incredibly powerful sales mechanism because they check MOST of the boxes necessary for generating leads and sales.

A well executed webinar builds rapport with your prospect, establishes your authority as an expert or trusted voice, and allows you to really explain the value and benefits of your offer.

Time and frequency spent with people builds an invisible connection. And a good webinar is almost like sitting down for coffee with someone for an hour. By the end the viewer feels like they *know* you.

This is why webinars are extremely good at selling high ticket offers between $500-$2000 and all the way up to $5,000-$25,000 if they lead to a phone call.

In my case, the webinar functions as both a lead magnet *and* a sales pitch because the webinar itself provides valuable information while also offering my paid product.

The key is that when people register for my webinar they provide their email address. This allows me to start a conversation with them via email where I introduce myself, explore their problem, and offer my solution. It's a natural and relational business model.

Then, even if that person decides not to buy right then I can follow up with them and continue the conversation via email but those leads are way more qualified than someone who just grabbed a freebie lead magnet.

One distribution method I've used is a high quality webinar that introduces me and my product to my target audience.

At the end of the webinar there's an invitation to join my paid program. That's how I made most of my first sales and built my first list.

So, how does it work?

First, I run Facebook ads into targeted audiences calling out my ideal customer. In my case, it was pastors and church leaders that want help growing their churches.

Next, they go to a landing page where they can register for my webinar with their name and email. Boom! Now, I've got a lead for my business that I can build a relationship with and potentially do business with in the future.

Then, they watch my webinar that teaches them about church growth and at the end they have an opportunity to purchase my course.

Product and Distribution. Simple!

There are lots of popular webinar models like the "Perfect" webinar model or the "Hero's Journey" but here's a simple framework for you to use:

1) **Intro - Title -** Here's what you'll learn…agitate the problem you're solving or build excitement for the content you're teaching, future pace: imagine this…imagine that…

2) **Story** - Tell your story, build authority, but for goodness sake make it quick…people don't care about you…they care about their problem or desire…

3) **Content** - You can frame this as 3 secrets or truths or whatever…don't hard teach…give them the *what* but not the *how*…

4) **Offer** - Transition with, "Can I tell you about how we can work together if you'd like to go deeper? Then, quickly introduce your offer and make sure you turn features into benefits.

5) **Close** - Give people a compelling reason to buy and buy NOW. Use a deadline or promotion.

Again, webinars (live or automated) are a powerful way to connect with people.

If you're starting out I highly recommend running at a least a few live webinars where you deliver your content (big idea and the *"What"* of your solution) and pitch your "no-brainer" offer.

This will give you invaluable experience and connect you with real-time feedback from your market. Plus, it can make you some quick cash to build up your business.

Here's a quick rundown:

1) Run an ad inviting people to register for your live (automated) webinar.

2) Collect emails and send a few to "warm" them up before the scheduled time.

3) Host your webinar and make your offer.

4) Follow up via email (I'd create a 5-7 day sequence that delivers automatically) to make a few more sales!

5) Close the offer, put the remaining leads on your broadcast list, and rinse/repeat.

Russel Brunson once said that if he was starting from scratch and wanted to make a million dollars in a year he'd do a live webinar once a week!

Might just be something to consider…

You can visit…

www.boringoldbusiness.com/tools

…to see my recommend webinar software.

That's about it! Good luck with your webinar!

APPENDIX 6: WHY I CHOSE TO PUT THIS TRAINING IN A PHYSICAL BOOK

Hopefully you followed instructions and didn't immediately come to this appendix but you probably did anyways. Can't follow instructions can ya? Let me spill the beans. The reason I put this content into a physical book is because…

- It's tangible and that psychologically equates with value.
- It boosts authority. *Published author anyone? Self-published but still…*(actually self-publishing and selling your own book is WAY smarter for almost everyone…)
- Sending you a book allowed me to send you a "ride-along" which is an ad insert or brochure for another product. Really profitable and valuable.
- It's harder to copy and pirate than an eBook. I'm not really worried about this because if you're pirating me I'm popular…but it does add a layer of protection.
- It will live on your shelf, coffee table, nightstand, or bathroom counter reminding you of me! Kinda gross…but it's good for business.
- There's wisdom in being multi-faceted. I don't only use one

medium. I have video, audio, eBook, audiobook, etc and now physical books...
- And probably the BIGGEST and most important reason of them all. *Drum roll please*...it's been scientifically proven that our brains respond differently to the stimulus of reading a physical book. And this is highly valuable information that I fully expect you to implement and make money from. That's the whole point of the book! So I did what I thought was best FOR YOU. You're welcome.
- Those are just a few reasons why I chose the physical book medium for this content...now GET BACK TO READING!

NEXT STEPS

For more resources and training visit:

www.BoringOldBusiness.com

- Subscribe to the email list for ongoing business, sales, and marketing training.
- Get coaching in the monthly membership.
- Discover other books and courses that will help you grow your business!

Have a great day!

Jake Schmelzer